The Princes

Richard Harding Davis

Alpha Editions

This edition published in 2024

ISBN 9789362095350

Design and Setting By

Alpha Editions

www.alphaedis.com

Email - info@alphaedis.com

Contents

I

H. R. H. the Princess Aline of Hohenwald came into the life of Morton Carlton--or "Morney" Carlton, as men called him--of New York city, when that young gentleman's affairs and affections were best suited to receive her. Had she made her appearance three years sooner or three years later, it is quite probable that she would have passed on out of his life with no more recognition from him than would have been expressed in a look of admiring curiosity.

But coming when she did, when his time and heart were both unoccupied, she had an influence upon young Mr. Carlton which led him into doing several wise and many foolish things, and which remained with him always. Carlton had reached a point in his life, and very early in his life, when he could afford to sit at ease and look back with modest satisfaction to what he had forced himself to do, and forward with pleasurable anticipations to whatsoever he might choose to do in the future. The world had appreciated what he had done, and had put much to his credit, and he was prepared to draw upon this grandly.

At the age of twenty he had found himself his own master, with excellent family connections, but with no family, his only relative being a bachelor uncle, who looked at life from the point of view of the Union Club's windows, and who objected to his nephew's leaving Harvard to take up the study of art in Paris. In that city (where at Julian's he was nicknamed the junior Carlton, for the obvious reason that he was the older of the two Carltons in the class, and because he was well dressed) he had shown himself a harder worker than others who were less careful of their appearance and of their manners. His work, of which he did not talk, and his ambitions, of which he also did not talk, bore fruit early, and at twenty-six he had become a portrait-painter of international reputation. Then the French government purchased one of his paintings at an absurdly small figure, and placed it in the Luxembourg, from whence it would in time depart to be buried in the hall of some provincial city; and American millionaires, and English Lord Mayors, members of Parliament, and members of the Institute, masters of hounds in pink coats, and ambassadors in gold lace, and beautiful women of all nationalities and conditions sat before his easel. And so when he returned to New York he was welcomed with an enthusiasm which showed that his countrymen had feared that the artistic atmosphere of the Old World had stolen him from them forever. He was particularly silent, even at this date, about his work, and listened to what others had to say of it with much awe, not unmixed with some amusement, that it should be he who was capable of producing anything worthy of such praise. We have been told what the mother duck felt when her ugly duckling turned into a swan, but we have never considered how much the ugly duckling must have marvelled also.

"Carlton is probably the only living artist," a brother artist had said of him, "who fails to appreciate how great his work is." And on this being repeated to Carlton by a good-natured friend, he had replied cheerfully, "Well, I'm sorry, but it is certainly better to be the only one who doesn't appreciate it than to be the only one who does."

He had never understood why such a responsibility had been intrusted to him. It was, as he expressed it, not at all in his line, and young girls who sought to sit at the feet of the master found him making love to them in the most charming manner in the world, as though he were not entitled to all the rapturous admiration of their very young hearts, but had to sue for it like any ordinary mortal. Carlton always felt as though some day some one would surely come along and say: "Look here, young man, this talent doesn't belong to you; it's mine. What do you mean by pretending that such an idle good-natured youth as yourself is entitled to such a gift of genius?" He felt that he was keeping it in trust, as it were; that it had been changed at birth, and that the proper guardian would eventually relieve him of his treasure.

Personally Carlton was of the opinion that he should have been born in the active days of knights-errant--to have had nothing more serious to do than to ride abroad with a blue ribbon fastened to the point of his lance, and with the spirit to unhorse any one who objected to its color, or to the claims of superiority of the noble lady who had tied it there. There was not, in his opinion, at the present day any sufficiently pronounced method of declaring admiration for the many lovely women this world contained. A proposal of marriage he considered to be a mean and clumsy substitute for the older way, and was uncomplimentary to the many other women left unasked, and marriage itself required much more constancy than he could give. He had a most romantic and old-fashioned ideal of women as a class, and from the age of fourteen had been a devotee of hundreds of them as individuals; and though in that time his ideal had received several severe shocks, he still believed that the "not impossible she" existed somewhere, and his conscientious efforts to find out whether every women he met might not be that one had led him not unnaturally into many difficulties.

"The trouble with me is," he said, "that I care too much to make Platonic friendship possible, and don't care enough to marry any particular woman--that is, of course, supposing that any particular one would be so little particular as to be willing to marry me. How embarrassing it would be, now," he argued, "if, when you were turning away from the chancel after the ceremony, you should look at one of the bridesmaids and see the woman whom you really should have married! How distressing that would be! You couldn't very well stop and say: 'I am very sorry, my dear, but it seems I have made a mistake. That young woman on the right has a most interesting and beautiful face. I am very much afraid that she is the one.' It would be too late then; while now, in my free state, I can continue my search without any sense of responsibility."

"Why"--he would exclaim--"I have walked miles to get a glimpse of a beautiful woman in a suburban window, and time and time again when I have seen a face in a passing brougham I have pursued it in a hansom, and learned where the owner of the face lived, and spent weeks in finding some one to present me, only to discover that she was self-conscious or uninteresting or engaged. Still I had assured myself that she was not the one. I am very conscientious, and I consider that it is my duty to go so far with every woman I meet as to be able to learn whether she is or is not the one, and the sad result is that I am like a man who follows the hounds but is never in at the death."

"Well," some married woman would say, grimly, "I hope you will get your deserts some day; and you WILL, too. Some day some girl will make you suffer for this."

"Oh, that's all right," Carlton would answer, meekly. "Lots of women have made me suffer, if that's what you think I need."

"Some day," the married woman would prophesy, "you will care for a woman so much that you will have no eyes for any one else. That's the way it is when one is married."

"Well, when that's the way it is with ME," Carlton would reply, "I certainly hope to get married; but until it is, I think it is safer for all concerned that I should not."

Then Carlton would go to the club and complain bitterly to one of his friends.

"How unfair married women are!" he would say. "The idea of thinking a man could have no eyes but for one woman! Suppose I had never heard a note of music until I was twenty-five years of age, and was then given my hearing. Do you suppose my pleasure in music would make me lose my pleasure in everything else? Suppose I met and married a girl at twenty-five. Is that going to make me forget all the women I knew before I met her? I think not. As a matter of fact, I really deserve a great deal of credit for remaining single, for I am naturally very affectionate; but when I see what poor husbands my friends make, I prefer to stay as I am until I am sure that I will make a better one. It is only fair to the woman."

Carlton was sitting in the club alone. He had that sense of superiority over his fellows and of irresponsibility to the world about him that comes to a man when he knows that his trunks are being packed and that his state-room is engaged. He was leaving New York long before most of his friends could get away. He did not know just where he was going, and preferred not to know. He wished to have a complete holiday, and to see Europe as an idle tourist, and not as an artist with an eye to his own improvement. He had plenty of time and money; he was sure to run across friends in the big cities, and acquaintances he could make or not, as he pleased, en route. He was not sorry to go. His going would serve to put an end to what gossip there might be of his engagement to numerous young women whose admiration for him as an artist, he was beginning to fear, had taken on a more personal tinge. "I wish," he said, gloomily, "I didn't like people so well. It seems to cause them and me such a lot of trouble."

He sighed, and stretched out his hand for a copy of one of the English illustrated papers. It had a fresher interest to him because the next number of it that he would see would be in the city in which it was printed. The paper in his hands was the St. James Budget, and it contained much fashionable intelligence concerning the preparations for a royal wedding which was soon to take place between members of two of the reigning families of Europe. There was on one page a half-tone reproduction of a photograph, which showed a group of young people belonging to several of these reigning families, with their names and titles printed above and below the picture. They were princesses, archdukes, or grand-dukes, and they were dressed like young English men and women, and with no sign about them of their possible military or social rank.

One of the young princesses in the photograph was looking out of it and smiling in a tolerant, amused way, as though she had thought of something which she could not wait to enjoy until after the picture was taken. She was not posing consciously, as were some of the others, but was sitting in a natural attitude, with one arm over the back of her chair, and with her hands clasped before her. Her face was full of a fine intelligence and humor, and though one of the other princesses in the group was far more beautiful, this particular one had a much more high-bred air, and there was something of a challenge in her smile that made any one who looked at the picture smile also. Carlton studied the face for some time, and mentally approved of its beauty; the others seemed in comparison wooden and unindividual, but this one looked like a person he might have known, and whom he would certainly have liked. He turned the page and surveyed the features of the Oxford crew with lesser interest, and then turned the page again and gazed critically and severely at the face of the princess with the high-bred smile. He had hoped that he would find it less interesting at a second glance, but it did not prove to be so.

"'The Princess Aline of Hohenwald,'" he read. "She's probably engaged to one of those Johnnies beside her, and the Grand-Duke of Hohenwald behind her must be her brother." He put the paper down and went into luncheon, and diverted himself by mixing a salad dressing; but after a few moments he stopped in the midst of this employment, and told the waiter, with some unnecessary sharpness, to bring him the last copy of the St. James Budget.

"Confound it!" he added, to himself.

He opened the paper with a touch of impatience and gazed long and earnestly at the face of the Princess Aline, who continued to return his look with the same smile of amused tolerance. Carlton noted every detail of her tailor-made gown, of her high mannish collar, of her tie, and even the rings on her hand. There was nothing about her of which he could fairly disapprove. He wondered why it was that she could not have been born an approachable New York girl instead of a princess of a little German duchy, hedged in throughout her single life, and to be traded off eventually in marriage with as much consideration as though she were a princess of a real kingdom.

"She looks jolly too," he mused, in an injured tone; "and so very clever; and of course she has a beautiful complexion. All those German girls have. Your Royal Highness is more than pretty," he said, bowing his head gravely. "You look as a princess should look. I am sure it was one of your ancestors who discovered the dried pea under a dozen mattresses." He closed the paper, and sat for a moment with a perplexed smile of consideration. "Waiter," he exclaimed, suddenly, "send a messenger-boy to Brentano's for a copy of the St. James Budget, and bring me the Almanach de Gotha from the library. It is a little fat red book on the table near the window." Then Carlton opened the paper again and propped it up against a carafe, and continued his critical survey of the Princess Aline. He seized the Almanach, when it came, with some eagerness.

"Hohenwald (Maison de Grasse)," he read, and in small type below it:

"1. Ligne cadette (regnante) grand-ducale: Hohenwald et de Grasse.

"Guillaume-Albert-Frederick-Charles-Louis, Grand-Duc de Hohenwald et de Grasse, etc., etc., etc."

"That's the brother, right enough," muttered Carlton.

And under the heading "Soeurs" he read:

"4. Psse Aline.--Victoria-Beatrix-Louise-Helene, Alt. Gr.-Duc. Nee a Grasse, Juin, 1872."

"Twenty-two years old," exclaimed Carlton. "What a perfect age! I could not have invented a better one." He looked from the book to the face before him. "Now, my dear young lady," he said, "I know all about YOU. You live at Grasse, and you are connected, to judge by your names, with all the English royalties; and very pretty names they are, too--Aline, Helene, Victoria, Beatrix. You must be much more English than you are German; and I suppose you live in a little old castle, and your brother has a standing army of twelve men, and some day you are to marry a Russian Grand-Duke, or whoever your brother's Prime Minister--if he has a Prime Minister--decides is best for the politics of your little toy kingdom. Ah! to think," exclaimed Carlton, softly, "that such a lovely and glorious creature as that should be sacrificed for so insignificant a thing as the peace of Europe when she might make some young man happy?"

He carried a copy of the paper to his room, and cut the picture of the group out of the page and pasted it carefully on a stiff piece of card-board. Then he placed it on his dressing-table, in front of a photograph of a young woman in a large silver frame--which was a sign, had the young woman but known it, that her reign for the time being was over.

Nolan, the young Irishman who "did for" Carlton, knew better than to move it when he found it there. He had learned to study his master since he had joined him in London, and understood that one photograph in the silver frame was entitled to more consideration than three others on the writing-desk or half a dozen on the mantel-piece. Nolan had seen them come and go; he had watched them rise and fall; he had carried notes to them, and books and flowers; and had helped to dispose them from the silver frame and move them on by degrees down the line, until they went ingloriously into the big brass bowl on the side table. Nolan approved highly of this last choice. He did not know which one of the three in the group it might be; but they were all pretty, and their social standing was certainly distinguished.

Guido, the Italian model who ruled over the studio, and Nolan were busily packing when Carlton entered. He always said that Guido represented him in his professional and Nolan in his social capacity. Guido cleaned the brushes and purchased the artists' materials; Nolan cleaned his riding-boots and bought his theatre and railroad tickets.

"Guido," said Carlton, "there are two sketches I made in Germany last year, one of the Prime Minister, and one of Ludwig the actor; get them out for me, will you, and pack them for shipping. Nolan," he went on, "here is a telegram to send."

Nolan would not have read a letter, but he looked upon telegrams as public documents, the reading of them as part of his perquisites. This one was addressed to Oscar Von Holtz, First Secretary, German Embassy, Washington, D.C., and the message read:

"Please telegraph me full title and address
Princess Aline of Hohenwald. Where would a
letter reach her?

"MORTON CARLTON."

The next morning Nolan carried to the express office a box containing two oil-paintings on small canvases. They were addressed to the man in London who attended to the shipping and forwarding of Carlton's pictures in that town.

There was a tremendous crowd on the New York. She sailed at the obliging hour of eleven in the morning, and many people, in consequence, whose affection would not have stood in the way of their breakfast, made it a point to appear and to say goodbye. Carlton, for his part, did not notice them; he knew by experience that the attractive-looking people always leave a steamer when the whistle blows, and that the next most attractive-looking, who remain on board, are ill all the way over. A man that he knew seized him by the arm as he was entering his cabin, and asked if he were crossing or just seeing people off.

"Well, then, I want to introduce you to Miss Morris and her aunt, Mrs. Downs; they are going over, and I should be glad if you would be nice to them. But you know her, I guess?" he asked, over his shoulder, as Carlton pushed his way after him down the deck.

"I know who she is," he said.

Miss Edith Morris was surrounded by a treble circle of admiring friends, and seemed to be holding her own. They all stopped when Carlton came up, and looked at him rather closely, and those whom he knew seemed to mark the fact by a particularly hearty greeting. The man who had brought him up acted as though he had successfully accomplished a somewhat difficult and creditable feat. Carlton bowed himself away, leaving Miss Morris to her friends, and saying that she would probably have to see him later, whether she wished it or not. He then went to meet the aunt, who received him kindly, for there were very few people on the passenger list, and she was glad they were to have his company. Before he left she introduced him to a young man named Abbey, who was hovering around her most anxiously, and whose interest, she seemed to think it necessary to explain, was due to the fact that he was engaged to Miss Morris. Mr. Abbey left the steamer when the whistle blew, and Carlton looked after him gratefully. He always enjoyed meeting attractive girls who were engaged, as it left him no choice in the matter, and excused him from finding out whether or not that particular young woman was the one.

Mrs. Downs and her niece proved to be experienced sailors, and faced the heavy sea that met the New York outside of Sandy Hook with unconcern. Carlton joined them, and they stood together leaning with their backs to the rail, and trying to fit the people who flitted past them to the names on the passenger list.

"The young lady in the sailor suit," said Miss Morris, gazing at the top of the smoke-stack, "is Miss Kitty Flood, of Grand Rapids. This is her first voyage, and she thinks a steamer is something like a yacht, and dresses for the part accordingly. She does not know that it is merely a moving hotel."

"I am afraid," said Carlton, "to judge from her agitation, that hers is going to be what the professionals call a 'dressing-room' part. Why is it," he asked, "that the girls on a steamer who wear gold anchors and the men in yachting-caps are always the first to disappear? That man with the sombrero," he went on, "is James M. Pollock, United States Consul to Mauritius; he is going out to his post. I know he is the consul, because he comes from Fort Worth, Texas, and is therefore admirably fitted to speak either French or the native language of the island."

"Oh, we don't send consuls to Mauritius," laughed Miss Morris. "Mauritius is one of those places from which you buy stamps, but no one really lives or goes there."

"Where are you going, may I ask?" inquired Carlton.

Miss Morris said that they were making their way to Constantinople and Athens, and then to Rome; that as they had not had the time to take the southern route, they purposed to journey across the Continent direct from Paris to the Turkish capital by the Orient Express.

"We shall be a few days in London, and in Paris only long enough for some clothes," she replied.

"The trousseau," thought Carlton. "Weeks is what she should have said."

The three sat together at the captain's table, and as the sea continued rough, saw little of either the captain or his other guests, and were thrown much upon the society of each other. They had innumerable friends and interests in common; and Mrs. Downs, who had been everywhere, and for long seasons at a time, proved as alive as her niece, and Carlton conceived a great liking for her. She seemed to be just and kindly minded, and, owing to her age, to combine the wider judgment of a man with the sympathetic interest of a woman. Sometimes they sat together in a row and read, and gossiped over what they read, or struggled up the deck as it rose and fell and buffeted with the wind; and later they gathered in a corner of the saloon and ate late suppers of Carlton's devising, or drank tea in the captain's cabin, which he had thrown open to them. They had started knowing much about one another, and this and the necessary proximity of the ship hastened their acquaintance.

The sea grew calmer the third day out, and the sun came forth and showed the decks as clean as bread-boards. Miss Morris and Carlton seated themselves on the huge iron riding-bits in the bow, and with their elbows on the rail looked down at the whirling blue water, and rejoiced silently in the steady rush of the great vessel, and in the uncertain warmth of the March sun. Carlton was sitting to leeward of Miss Morris, with a pipe between his teeth. He was warm, and at peace with the world. He had found his new acquaintance more than entertaining. She was even friendly, and treated him as though he were much her junior, as is the habit of young women lately married or who are about to be married. Carlton did not resent it; on the contrary, it made him more at his ease with her, and as she herself chose to treat him as a youth, he permitted himself to be as foolish as he pleased.

"I don't know why it is," he complained, peering over the rail, "but whenever I look over the side to watch the waves a man in a greasy cap always sticks his head out of a hole below me and scatters a barrelful of ashes or potato peelings all over the ocean. It spoils the effect for one. Next time he does it I am going to knock out the ashes of my pipe on the back of his neck." Miss Morris did not consider this worthy of comment, and there was a long lazy pause.

"You haven't told us where you go after London," she said; and then, without waiting for him to reply, she asked, "Is it your professional or your social side that you are treating to a trip this time?"

"Who told you that?" asked Carlton, smiling.

"Oh, I don't know. Some man. He said you were a Jekyll and Hyde. Which is Jekyll? You see, I only know your professional side."

"You must try to find out for yourself by deduction," he said, "as you picked out the other passengers. I am going to Grasse," he continued. "It's the capital of Hohenwald. Do you know it?"

"Yes," she said; "we were there once for a few days. We went to see the pictures. I suppose you know that the old Duke, the father of the present one, ruined himself almost by buying pictures for the Grasse gallery. We were there at a bad time, though, when the palace was closed to visitors, and the gallery too. I suppose that is what is taking you there?"

"No," Carlton said, shaking his head. "No, it is not the pictures. I am going to Grasse," he said, gravely, "to see the young woman with whom I am in love."

Miss Morris looked up in some surprise, and smiled consciously, with a natural feminine interest in an affair of love, and one which was a secret as well.

"Oh," she said, "I beg your pardon; we--I had not heard of it."

"No, it is not a thing one could announce exactly," said Carlton; "it is rather in an embryo state as yet--in fact, I have not met the young lady so far, but I mean to meet her. That's why I am going abroad."

Miss Morris looked at him sharply to see if he were smiling, but he was, on the contrary, gazing sentimentally at the horizon-line, and puffing meditatively on his pipe. He was apparently in earnest, and waiting for her to make some comment.

"How very interesting!" was all she could think to say.

"Yes, when you know the details, it is,----VERY interesting," he answered. "She is the Princess Aline of Hohenwald," he explained, bowing his head as though he were making the two young ladies known to one another. "She has several other names, six in all, and her age is twenty-two. That is all I know about her. I saw her picture in an illustrated paper just before I sailed, and I made up my mind I would meet her, and here I am. If she is not in Grasse, I intend to follow her to wherever she may be." He waved his pipe at the ocean before him, and recited, with mock seriousness:

"'Across the hills and far away,
Beyond their utmost purple rim,
And deep into the dying day,
The happy Princess followed him.'

"Only in this case, you see," said Carlton, "I am following the happy Princess."

"No; but seriously, though," said Miss Morris, "what is it you mean? Are you going to paint her portrait?"

"I never thought of that," exclaimed Carlton. "I don't know but what your idea is a good one. Miss Morris, that's a great idea." He shook his head approvingly. "I did not do wrong to confide in you," he said. "It was perhaps taking a liberty; but as you have not considered it as such, I am glad I spoke."

"But you don't really mean to tell me," exclaimed the girl, facing about, and nodding her head at him, "that you are going abroad after a woman whom you have never seen, and because you like a picture of her in a paper?"

"I do," said Carlton. "Because I like her picture, and because she is a Princess."

"Well, upon my word," said Miss Morris, gazing at him with evident admiration, "that's what my younger brother would call a distinctly sporting proposition. Only I don't see," she added, "what her being a Princess has to do with it."

"You don't?" laughed Carlton, easily. "That's the best part of it--that's the plot. The beauty of being in love with a Princess, Miss Morris," he said, "lies in the fact that you can't marry her; that you can love her deeply and forever, and nobody will ever come to you and ask your intentions, or hint that after such a display of affection you ought to do something. Now, with a girl who is not a Princess, even if she understands the situation herself, and wouldn't marry you to save her life, still there is always some one--a father, or a mother, or one of your friends--who makes it his business to interfere, and talks about it, and bothers you both. But with a Princess, you see, that is all eliminated. You can't marry a Princess, because they won't let you. A Princess has got to marry a real royal chap, and so you are perfectly ineligible and free to sigh for her, and make pretty speeches to her, and see her as often as you can, and revel in your devotion and unrequited affection."

Miss Morris regarded him doubtfully. She did not wish to prove herself too credulous. "And you honestly want me, Mr. Carlton, to believe that you are going abroad just for this?"

"You see," Carlton answered her, "if you only knew me better you would have no doubt on the subject at all. It isn't the thing some men would do, I admit, but it is exactly what any one who knows me would expect of me. I should describe it, having had acquaintance with the young man for some time, as being eminently characteristic. And besides, think what a good story it makes! Every other man who goes abroad this summer will try to tell about his travels when he gets back to New York, and, as usual, no one will listen to him. But they will HAVE to listen to me. 'You've been across since I saw you last. What did you do?' they'll ask, politely. And then, instead of simply telling them that I have been in Paris or London, I can say, 'Oh, I've been chasing around the globe after the Princess Aline of Hohenwald.' That sounds interesting, doesn't it? When you come to think of it," Carlton continued, meditatively, "it is not so very remarkable. Men go all the way to Cuba and Mexico, and even to India, after orchids, after a nasty flower that grows in an absurd way on the top of a tree. Why shouldn't a young man go as far as Germany after a beautiful Princess, who walks on the ground, and who can talk and think and feel? She is much more worth while than an orchid."

Miss Morris laughed indulgently. "Well, I didn't know such devotion existed at this end of the century," she said; "it's quite nice and encouraging. I hope you will succeed, I am sure. I only wish we were going to be near enough to see how you get on. I have never been a confidante when there was a real Princess concerned," she said; "it makes it so much more amusing. May one ask what your plans are?"

Carlton doubted if he had any plans as yet. "I have to reach the ground first," he said, "and after that I must reconnoitre. I may possibly adopt your idea, and ask to paint her portrait, only I dislike confusing my social and professional sides. As a matter of fact, though," he said, after a pause, laughing guiltily, "I have done a little of that already. I prepared her, as it were, for my coming. I sent her studies of two pictures I made last winter in Berlin. One of the Prime Minister, and one of Ludwig, the tragedian at the Court Theatre. I sent them to her through my London agent, so that she would think they had come from some one of her English friends, and I told the dealer not to let any one know who had forwarded them. My idea was that it might help me, perhaps, if she knew something about me before I appeared in person. It was a sort of letter of introduction written by myself."

"Well, really," expostulated Miss Morris, "you certainly woo in a royal way. Are you in the habit of giving away your pictures to any one whose photograph you happen to like? That seems to me to be giving new lamps for old to a degree. I must see if I haven't some of my sister's photographs in my trunk. She is considered very beautiful."

"Well, you wait until you see this particular portrait, and--you will understand it better," said Carlton.

The steamer reached Southampton early in the afternoon, and Carlton secured a special compartment on the express to London for Mrs. Downs and her niece and himself, with one adjoining for their maid and Nolan. It was a beautiful day, and Carlton sat with his eyes fixed upon the passing fields and villages, exclaiming with pleasure from time to time at the white roads and the feathery trees and hedges, and the red roofs of the inns and square towers of the village churches.

"Hedges are better than barbed-wire fences, aren't they?" he said. "You see that girl picking wild flowers from one of them? She looks just as though she were posing for a picture for an illustrated paper. She couldn't pick flowers from a barbed-wire fence, could she? And there would probably be a tramp along the road somewhere to frighten her; and see--the chap in knickerbockers farther down the road leaning on the stile. I am sure he is waiting for her; and here comes a coach," he ran on. "Don't the red wheels look well against the hedges? It's a pretty little country, England, isn't it?--like a private park or a model village. I am glad to get back to it--I am glad to see the three-and-six signs with the little slanting dash between the shillings and pennies. Yes, even the steam-rollers and the man with the red flag in front are welcome."

"I suppose," said Mrs. Downs, "it's because one has been so long on the ocean that the ride to London seems so interesting. It always pays me for the entire trip. Yes," she said, with a sigh, "in spite of the patent-medicine signs they have taken to putting up all along the road. It seems a pity they should adopt our bad habits instead of our good ones."

"They are a bit slow at adopting anything," commented Carlton. "Did you know, Mrs. Downs, that electric lights are still as scarce in London as they are in Timbuctoo? Why, I saw an electric-light plant put up in a Western town in three days once; there were over a hundred burners in one saloon, and the engineer who put them up told me in confidence that--"

What the chief engineer told him in confidence was never disclosed, for at that moment Miss Morris interrupted him with a sudden sharp exclamation.

"Oh, Mr. Carlton," she exclaimed, breathlessly, "listen to this!" She had been reading one of the dozen papers which Carlton had purchased at the station, and was now shaking one of them at him, with her eyes fixed on the open page.

"My dear Edith," remonstrated her aunt, "Mr. Carlton was telling us--"

"Yes, I know," exclaimed Miss Morris, laughing, "but this interests him much more than electric lights. Who do you think is in London?" she cried, raising her eyes to his, and pausing for proper dramatic effect. "The Princess Aline of Hohenwald!"

"No?" shouted Carlton.

"Yes," Miss Morris answered, mocking his tone. "Listen. 'The Queen's Drawing-room'--em--e--m--'on her right was the Princess of Wales'--em--m. Oh, I can't find it--no--yes, here it is. 'Next to her stood the Princess Aline of Hohenwald. She wore a dress of white silk, with train of silver brocade trimmed with fur. Ornaments--emeralds and diamonds; orders--Victoria and Albert, jubilee Commemoration Medal, Coburg and Gotha, and Hohenwald and Grasse.'"

"By Jove!" cried Carlton, excitedly. "I say, is that really there? Let me see it, please, for myself."

Miss Morris handed him the paper, with her finger on the paragraph, and picking up another, began a search down its columns.

"You are right," exclaimed Carlton, solemnly; "it's she, sure enough. And here I've been within two hours of her and didn't know it?"

Miss Morris gave another triumphant cry, as though she had discovered a vein of gold.

"Yes, and here she is again," she said, "in the Gentlewoman: 'The Queen's dress was of black, as usual, but relieved by a few violet ribbons in the bonnet; and Princess Beatrice, who sat by her mother's side, showed but little trace of the anxiety caused by Princess Ena's accident. Princess Aline, on the front seat, in a light brown jacket and a becoming bonnet, gave the necessary touch to a picture which Londoners would be glad to look upon more often.'"

Carlton sat staring forward, with his hands on his knees, and with his eyes open wide from excitement. He presented so unusual an appearance of bewilderment and delight that Mrs. Downs looked at him and at her niece for some explanation. "The young lady seems to interest you," said she, tentatively.

"She is the most charming creature in the world, Mrs. Downs," cried Carlton, "and I was going all the way to Grasse to see her, and now it turns out that she is here in England, within a few miles of us." He turned and waved his hands at the passing landscape. "Every minute brings us nearer together."

"And you didn't feel it in the air!" mocked Miss Morris, laughing. "You are a pretty poor sort of a man to let a girl tell you where to find the woman you love."

Carlton did not answer, but stared at her very seriously and frowned intently. "Now I have got to begin all over again and readjust things," he said. "We might have guessed she would be in London, on account of this royal wedding. It is a great pity it isn't later in the season, when there would be more things going on and more chances of meeting her. Now they will all be interested in themselves, and, being extremely exclusive, no one who isn't a cousin to the bridegroom or an Emperor would have any chance at all. Still, I can see her! I can look at her, and that's something."

"It is better than a photograph, anyway," said Miss Morris.

"They will be either at Buckingham Palace or at Windsor, or they will stop at Brown's," said Carlton. "All royalties go to Brown's. I don't know why, unless it is because it is so expensive; or maybe it is expensive because royalties go there; but, in any event, if they are not at the palace, that is where they will be, and that is where I shall have to go too."

When the train drew up at Victoria Station, Carlton directed Nolan to take his things to Brown's Hotel, but not to unload them until he had arrived. Then he drove with the ladies to Cox's, and saw them settled there. He promised to return at once to dine, and to tell them what he had discovered in his absence. "You've got to help me in this, Miss Morris," he said, nervously. "I am beginning to feel that I am not worthy of her."

"Oh yes, you are!" she said, laughing; "but don't forget that 'it's not the lover who comes to woo, but the lover's WAY of wooing,' and that 'faint heart'--and the rest of it."

"Yes, I know," said Carlton, doubtfully; "but it's a bit sudden, isn't it?"

"Oh, I am ashamed of you! You are frightened."

"No, not frightened, exactly," said the painter. "I think it's just natural emotion."

As Carlton turned into Albemarle Street he noticed a red carpet stretching from the doorway of Brown's Hotel out across the sidewalk to a carriage, and a bareheaded man bustling about apparently assisting several gentlemen to get into it. This and another carriage and Nolan's four-wheeler blocked the way; but without waiting for them to move up, Carlton leaned out of his hansom and called the bareheaded man to its side.

"Is the Duke of Hohenwald stopping at your hotel?" he asked. The bareheaded man answered that he was.

"All right, Nolan," cried Carlton. "They can take in the trunks."

Hearing this, the bareheaded man hastened to help Carlton to alight. "That was the Duke who just drove off, sir; and those," he said, pointing to three muffled figures who were stepping into a second carriage, "are his sisters, the Princesses."

Carlton stopped midway, with one foot on the step and the other in the air.

"The deuce they are!" he exclaimed; "and which is--" he began, eagerly, and then remembering himself, dropped back on the cushions of the hansom.

He broke into the little dining-room at Cox's in so excited a state that two dignified old gentlemen who were eating there sat open-mouthed in astonished disapproval. Mrs. Downs and Miss Morris had just come down stairs.

"I have seen her!" Carlton cried, ecstatically; "only half an hour in the town, and I've seen her already!"

"No, really?" exclaimed Miss Morris. "And how did she look? Is she as beautiful as you expected?"

"Well, I can't tell yet," Carlton answered.

"There were three of them, and they were all muffled up, and which one of the three she was I don't know. She wasn't labelled, as in the picture, but she was there, and I saw her. The woman I love was one of that three, and I have engaged rooms at the hotel, and this very night the same roof shelters us both."

II

"The course of true love certainly runs smoothly with you," said Miss Morris, as they seated themselves at the table. "What is your next move? What do you mean to do now?"

"The rest is very simple," said Carlton. "To-morrow morning I will go to the Row; I will be sure to find some one there who knows all about them--where they are going, and who they are seeing, and what engagements they may have. Then it will only be a matter of looking up some friend in the Household or in one of the embassies who can present me."

"Oh," said Miss Morris, in the tone of keenest disappointment, "but that is such a commonplace ending! You started out so romantically. Couldn't you manage to meet her in a less conventional way?"

"I am afraid not," said Carlton. "You see, I want to meet her very much, and to meet her very soon, and the quickest way of meeting her, whether it's romantic or not, isn't a bit too quick for me. There will be romance enough after I am presented, if I have my way."

But Carlton was not to have his way; for he had overlooked the fact that it requires as many to make an introduction as a bargain, and he had left the Duke of Hohenwald out of his considerations. He met many people he knew in the Row the next morning; they asked him to lunch, and brought their horses up to the rail, and he patted the horses' heads, and led the conversation around to the royal wedding, and through it to the Hohenwalds. He learned that they had attended a reception at the German Embassy on the previous night, and it was one of the secretaries of that embassy who informed him of their intended departure that morning on the eleven o'clock train to Paris.

"To Paris!" cried Carlton, in consternation. "What! all of them?"

"Yes, all of them, of course. Why?" asked the young German. But Carlton was already dodging across the tan-bark to Piccadilly and waving his stick at a hansom.

Nolan met him at the door of Brown's Hotel with an anxious countenance.

"Their Royal Highnesses have gone, sir," he said. "But I've packed your trunks and sent them to the station. Shall I follow them, sir?"

"Yes," said Carlton. "Follow the trunks and follow the Hohenwalds. I will come over on the Club train at four. Meet me at the station, and tell me to what hotel they have gone. Wait; if I miss you, you can find me at the Hotel Continental; but if they go straight on through Paris, you go with them, and telegraph me here and to the Continental. Telegraph at every station, so I can keep track of you. Have you enough money?"

"I have, sir--enough for a long trip, sir."

"Well, you'll need it," said Carlton, grimly. "This is going to be a long trip. It is twenty minutes to eleven now; you will have to hurry. Have you paid my bill here?"

"I have, sir," said Nolan.

"Then get off, and don't lose sight of those people again."

Carlton attended to several matters of business, and then lunched with Mrs. Downs and her niece. He had grown to like them very much, and was sorry to lose sight of them, but consoled himself by thinking he would see them a few days at least in Paris. He judged that he would be there for some time, as he did not think the Princess Aline and her sisters would pass through that city without stopping to visit the shops on the Rue de la Paix.

"All women are not princesses," he argued, "but all princesses are women."

"We will be in Paris on Wednesday," Mrs. Downs told him. "The Orient Express leaves there twice a week, on Mondays and Thursdays, and we have taken an apartment for next Thursday, and will go right on to Constantinople."

"But I thought you said you had to buy a lot of clothes there?" Carlton expostulated.

Mrs. Downs said that they would do that on their way home.

Nolan met Carlton at the station, and told him that he had followed the Hohenwalds to the Hotel Meurice. "There is the Duke, sir, and the three Princesses," Nolan said, "and there are two German gentlemen acting as equerries, and an English captain, a sort of A.D.C. to the Duke, and two elderly ladies, and eight servants. They travel very simple, sir, and their people are in undress livery. Brown and red, sir."

Carlton pretended not to listen to this. He had begun to doubt but that Nolan's zeal would lead him into some indiscretion, and would end disastrously to himself. He spent the evening alone in front of the Cafe de la Paix, pleasantly occupied in watching the life and movement of that great meeting of the highways. It did not seem possible that he had ever been away. It was as though he had picked up a book and opened it at the page and place at which he had left off reading it a moment before. There was the same type, the same plot, and the same characters, who were doing the same characteristic things. Even the waiter who tipped out his coffee knew him; and he knew, or felt as though he knew, half of those who passed, or who shared with him the half of the sidewalk. The women at the next table considered the slim, good-looking young American with friendly curiosity, and the men with them discussed him in French, until a well-known Parisian recognized Carlton in passing, and hailed him joyously in the same language, at which the women laughed and the men looked sheepishly conscious.

On the following morning Carlton took up his post in the open court of the Meurice, with his coffee and the Figaro to excuse his loitering there. He had not been occupied with these over-long before Nolan approached him, in some excitement, with the information that their Royal Highnesses--as he delighted to call them--were at that moment "coming down the lift."

Carlton could hear their voices, and wished to step around the corner and see them; it was for this chance he had been waiting; but he could not afford to act in so undignified a manner before Nolan, so he merely crossed his legs nervously, and told the servant to go back to the rooms.

"Confound him!" he said; "I wish he would let me conduct my own affairs in my own way. If I don't stop him, he'll carry the Princess Aline off by force and send me word where he has hidden her."

The Hohenwalds had evidently departed for a day's outing, as up to five o'clock they had not returned; and Carlton, after loitering all the afternoon, gave up waiting for them, and went out to dine at Laurent's, in the Champs Elysees. He had finished his dinner, and was leaning luxuriously forward, with his elbows on the table, and knocking the cigar ashes into his coffee-cup. He was pleasantly content. The trees hung heavy with leaves over his head, a fountain played and overflowed at his elbow, and the lamps of the fiacres passing and repassing on the Avenue of the Champs Elysees shone like giant fire-flies through the foliage. The touch of the gravel beneath his feet emphasized the free, out-of-door charm of the place, and the faces of the others around him looked more than usually cheerful in the light of the candles flickering under the clouded shades. His mind had gone back to his earlier student days in Paris, when life always looked as it did now in the brief half-hour of satisfaction which followed a cold bath or a good dinner, and he had forgotten himself and his surroundings. It was the voices of the people at the table behind him that brought him back to the present moment. A man was talking; he spoke in English, with an accent.

"I should like to go again through the Luxembourg," he said; "but you need not be bound by what I do."

"I think it would be pleasanter if we all keep together," said a girl's voice, quietly. She also spoke in English, and with the same accent.

The people whose voices had interrupted him were sitting and standing around a long table, which the waiters had made large enough for their party by placing three of the smaller ones side by side; they had finished their dinner, and the women, who sat with their backs towards Carlton, were pulling on their gloves.

"Which is it to be, then?" said the gentleman, smiling. "The pictures or the dressmakers?"

The girl who had first spoken turned to the one next to her.

"Which would you rather do, Aline?" she asked.

Carlton moved so suddenly that the men behind him looked at him curiously; but he turned, nevertheless, in his chair and faced them, and in order to excuse his doing so beckoned to one of the waiters. He was within two feet of the girl who had been called "Aline." She raised her head to speak, and saw Carlton staring open-eyed at her. She glanced at him for an instant, as if to assure herself that she did not know him, and then, turning to her brother, smiled in the same tolerant, amused way in which she had so often smiled upon Carlton from the picture.

"I am afraid I had rather go to the Bon March," she said.

One of the waiters stepped in between them, and Carlton asked him for his bill; but when it came he left it lying on the plate, and sat staring out into the night between the candles, puffing sharply on his cigar, and recalling to his memory his first sight of the Princess Aline of Hohenwald.

That night, as he turned into bed, he gave a comfortable sigh of content. "I am glad she chose the dressmakers instead of the pictures," he said.

Mrs. Downs and Miss Morris arrived in Paris on Wednesday, and expressed their anxiety to have Carlton lunch with them, and to hear him tell of the progress of his love-affair. There was not much to tell; the Hohenwalds had come and gone from the hotel as freely as any other tourists in Paris, but the very lack of ceremony about their movements was in itself a difficulty. The manner of acquaintance he could make in the court of the Hotel Meurice with one of the men over a cup of coffee or a glass of bock would be as readily discontinued as begun, and for his purpose it would have been much better if the Hohenwalds had been living in state with a visitors' book and a chamberlain.

On Wednesday evening Carlton took the ladies to the opera, where the Hohenwalds occupied a box immediately opposite them. Carlton pretended to be surprised at this fact, but Mrs. Downs doubted his sincerity.

"I saw Nolan talking to their courier to-day," she said, "and I fancy he asked a few leading questions."

"Well, he didn't learn much if he did," he said. "The fellow only talks German."

"Ah, then he has been asking questions!" said Miss Morris.

"Well, he does it on his own responsibility," said Carlton, "for I told him to have nothing to do with servants. He has too much zeal, has Nolan; I'm afraid of him."

"If you were only half as interested as he is," said Miss Morris, "you would have known her long ago."

"Long ago?" exclaimed Carlton. "I only saw her four days since."

"She is certainly very beautiful," said Miss Morris, looking across the auditorium.

"But she isn't there," said Carlton.

"That's the eldest sister; the two other sisters went out on the coach this morning to Versailles, and were too tired to come tonight. At least, so Nolan says. He seems to have established a friendship for their English maid, but whether it's on my account or his own I don't know. I doubt his unselfishness."

"How disappointing of her!" said Miss Morris. "And after you had selected a box just across the way, too. It is such a pity to waste it on us." Carlton smiled, and looked up at her impudently, as though he meant to say something; but remembering that she was engaged to be married, changed his mind, and lowered his eyes to his programme.

"Why didn't you say it?" asked Miss Morris, calmly, turning her glass to the stage. "Wasn't it pretty?"

"No," said Carlton--"not pretty enough."

The ladies left the hotel the next day to take the Orient Express, which left Paris at six o'clock. They had bidden Carlton goodbye at four the same afternoon, and as he had come to their rooms for that purpose, they were in consequence a little surprised to see him at the station, running wildly along the platform, followed by Nolan and a porter. He came into their compartment after the train had started, and shook his head sadly at them from the door.

"Well, what do you think of this?" he said. "You can't get rid of me, you see. I'm going with you."

"Going with us?" asked Mrs. Downs. "How far?"

Carlton laughed, and, coming inside, dropped onto the cushions with a sigh. "I don't know," he said, dejectedly. "All the way, I'm afraid. That is, I mean, I'm very glad I am to have your society for a few days more; but really I didn't bargain for this."

"You don't mean to tell me that THEY are on this train?" said Miss Morris.

"They are," said Carlton. "They have a car to themselves at the rear. They only made up their minds to go this morning, and they nearly succeeded in giving me the slip again; but it seems that their English maid stopped Nolan in the hall to bid him good-bye, and so he found out their plans. They are going direct to Constantinople, and then to Athens. They had meant to stay in Paris two weeks longer, it seems, but they changed their minds last night. It was a very close shave for me. I only got back to the hotel in time to hear from the concierge that Nolan had flown with all of my things, and left word for me to follow. Just fancy! Suppose I had missed the train, and had had to chase him clear across the continent of Europe with not even a razor--"

"I am glad," said Miss Morris, "that Nolan has not taken a fancy to ME. I doubt if I could resist such impetuosity."

The Orient Express, in which Carlton and the mistress of his heart and fancy were speeding towards the horizon's utmost purple rim, was made up of six cars, one dining-car with a smoking-apartment attached, and five sleeping-cars, including the one reserved for the Duke of Hohenwald and his suite. These cars were lightly built, and rocked in consequence, and the dust raised by the rapid movement of the train swept through cracks and open windows, and sprinkled the passengers with a fine and irritating coating of soot and earth. There was one servant to the entire twenty-two passengers. He spoke eight languages, and never slept; but as his services were in demand by several people in as many different cars at the same moment he satisfied no one, and the complaint-box in the smoking-car was stuffed full to the slot in consequence before they had crossed the borders of France.

Carlton and Miss Morris went out upon one of the platforms and sat down upon a tool-box. "It's isn't as comfortable here as in an observation-car at home," said Carlton, "but it's just as noisy."

He pointed out to her from time to time the peasants gathering twigs, and the blue-bloused gendarmes guarding the woods and the fences skirting them. "Nothing is allowed to go to waste in this country," he said. "It looks as though they went over it once a month with a lawn-mower and a pruning-knife. I believe they number the trees as we number the houses."

"And did you notice the great fortifications covered with grass?" she said. "We have passed such a lot of them."

Carlton nodded.

"And did you notice that they all faced only one way?"

Carlton laughed, and nodded again. "Towards Germany," he said.

By the next day they had left the tall poplars and white roads behind them, and were crossing the land of low shiny black helmets and brass spikes. They had come into a country of low mountains and black forests, with old fortified castles topping the hills, and with red-roofed villages scattered around the base.

"How very military it all is!" Mrs. Downs said. "Even the men at the lonely little stations in the forests wear uniforms; and do you notice how each of them rolls up his red flag and holds it like a sword, and salutes the train as it passes?"

They spent the hour during which the train shifted from one station in Vienna to the other driving about in an open carriage, and stopped for a few moments in front of a cafe to drink beer and to feel solid earth under them again, returning to the train with a feeling which was almost that of getting back to their own rooms. Then they came to great steppes covered with long thick grass, and flooded in places with little lakes of broken ice; great horned cattle stood knee-deep in this grass, and at the villages and way-stations were people wearing sheepskin jackets and waistcoats covered with silver buttons. In one place there was a wedding procession waiting for the train to pass, with the friends of the bride and groom in their best clothes, the women with silver breastplates, and boots to their knees. It seemed hardly possible that only two days before they had seen another wedding party in the Champs Elysees, where the men wore evening dress, and the women were bareheaded and with long trains. In forty-eight hours they had passed through republics, principalities, empires, and kingdoms, and from spring to winter. It was like walking rapidly over a painted panorama of Europe.

On the second evening Carlton went off into the smoking-car alone. The Duke of Hohenwald and two of his friends had finished a late supper, and were seated in the apartment adjoining it. The Duke was a young man with a heavy beard and eyeglasses. He was looking over an illustrated catalogue of the Salon, and as Carlton dropped on the sofa opposite the Duke raised his head and looked at him curiously, and then turned over several pages of the catalogue and studied one of them, and then back at Carlton, as though he were comparing him with something on the page before him. Carlton was looking out at the night, but he could follow what was going forward, as it was reflected in the glass of the car window. He saw the Duke hand the catalogue to one of the equerries, who raised his eyebrows and nodded his head in assent. Carlton wondered what this might mean, until he remembered that there was a portrait of himself by a French artist in the Salon, and concluded it had been reproduced in the catalogue. He could think of nothing else which would explain the interest the two men showed in him. On the morning following he sent Nolan out to purchase a catalogue at the first station at which they stopped, and found that his guess was a correct one. A portrait of himself had been reproduced in black and white, with his name below it.

"Well, they know who I am now," he said to Miss Morris, "even if they don't know me. That honor is still in store for them."

"I wish they did not lock themselves up so tightly," said Miss Morris. "I want to see her very much. Cannot we walk up and down the platform at the next station? She may be at the window."

"Of course," said Carlton. "You could have seen her at Buda-Pesth if you had spoken of it. She was walking up and down then. The next time the train stops we will prowl up and down and feast our eyes upon her."

But Miss Morris had her wish gratified without that exertion. The Hohenwalds were served in the dining-car after the other passengers had finished, and were in consequence only to be seen when they passed by the doors of the other compartments. But this same morning, after luncheon, the three Princesses, instead of returning to their own car, seated themselves in the compartment adjoining the dining-car, while the men of their party lit their cigars and sat in a circle around them.

"I was wondering how long they could stand three men smoking in one of the boxes they call cars," said Mrs. Downs. She was seated between Miss Morris and Carlton, directly opposite the Hohenwalds, and so near them that she had to speak in a whisper. To avoid doing this Miss Morris asked Carlton for a pencil, and scribbled with it in the novel she held on her lap. Then she passed them both back to him, and said, aloud: "Have you read this? It has such a pretty dedication." The dedication read, "Which is Aline?" And Carlton, taking the pencil in his turn, made a rapid sketch of her on the fly-leaf, and wrote beneath it: "This is she. Do you wonder I travelled four thousand miles to see her?"

Miss Morris took the book again, and glanced at the sketch, and then at the three Princesses, and nodded her head. "It is very beautiful," she said, gravely, looking out at the passing landscape.

"Well, not beautiful exactly," answered Carlton, surveying the hills critically, "but certainly very attractive. It is worth travelling a long way to see, and I should think one would grow very fond of it."

Miss Morris tore the fly-leaf out of the book, and slipped it between the pages. "May I keep it?" she said. Carlton nodded. "And will you sign it?" she asked, smiling. Carlton shrugged his shoulders, and laughed. "If you wish it," he answered.

The Princess wore a gray cheviot travelling dress, as did her sisters, and a gray Alpine hat. She was leaning back, talking to the English captain who accompanied them, and laughing. Carlton thought he had never seen a woman who appealed so strongly to every taste of which he was possessed. She seemed so sure of herself, so alert, and yet so gracious, so easily entertained, and yet, when she turned her eyes towards the strange, dismal landscape, so seriously intent upon its sad beauty. The English captain dropped his head, and with the pretence of pulling at his mustache, covered his mouth as he spoke to her. When he had finished he gazed consciously at the roof of the car, and she kept her eyes fixed steadily at the object towards which they had turned when he had ceased speaking, and then, after a decent pause, turned her eyes, as Carlton knew she would, towards him.

"He was telling her who I am," he thought, "and about the picture in the catalogue."

In a few moments she turned to her sister and spoke to her, pointing out at something in the scenery, and the same pantomime was repeated, and again with the third sister.

"Did you see those girls talking about you, Mr. Carlton?" Miss Morris asked, after they had left the car.

Carlton said it looked as though they were.

"Of course they were," said Miss Morris.

"That Englishman told the Princess Aline something about you, and then she told her sister, and she told the eldest one. It would be nice if they inherit their father's interest in painting, wouldn't it?"

"I would rather have it degenerate into an interest in painters myself," said Carlton.

Miss Morris discovered, after she had returned to her own car, that she had left the novel where she had been sitting, and Carlton sent Nolan back for it. It had slipped to the floor, and the fly-leaf upon which Carlton had sketched the Princess Aline was lying face down beside it. Nolan picked up the leaf, and saw the picture, and read the inscription below: "This is she. Do you wonder I travelled four thousand miles to see her?"

He handed the book to Miss Morris, and was backing out of the compartment, when she stopped him.

"There was a loose page in this, Nolan," she said. "It's gone; did you see it?"

"A loose page, miss?" said Nolan, with some concern. "Oh, yes, miss; I was going to tell you; there was a scrap of paper blew away when I was passing between the carriages. Was it something you wanted, miss?"

"Something I wanted!" exclaimed Miss Morris, in dismay.

Carlton laughed easily. "It is just as well I didn't sign it, after all," he said. "I don't want to proclaim my devotion to any Hungarian gypsy who happens to read English."

"You must draw me another, as a souvenir," Miss Morris said.

Nolan continued on through the length of the car until he had reached the one occupied by the Hohenwalds, where he waited on the platform until the English maidservant saw him and came to the door of the carriage.

"What hotel are your people going to stop at in Constantinople?" Nolan asked.

"The Grande-Bretagne, I think," she answered.

"That's right," said Nolan, approvingly. "That's the one we are going to. I thought I would come and tell you about it. And, by-the-way," he said, "here's a picture somebody's made of your Princess Aline. She dropped it, and I picked it up. You had better give it back to her. Well," he added, politely, "I'm glad you are coming to our hotel in Constantinople; it's pleasant having some one to talk to who can speak your own tongue."

The girl returned to the car, and left Nolan alone upon the platform. He exhaled a long breath of suppressed excitement, and then gazed around nervously upon the empty landscape.

"I fancy that's going to hurry things up a bit," he murmured, with an anxious smile; "he'd never get along at all if it wasn't for me."

For reasons possibly best understood by the German ambassador, the state of the Hohenwalds at Constantinople differed greatly from that which had obtained at the French capital. They no longer came and went as they wished, or wandered through the show-places of the city like ordinary tourists. There was, on the contrary, not only a change in their manner towards others, but there was an insistence on their part of a difference in the attitude of others towards themselves. This showed itself in the reserving of the half of the hotel for their use, and in the haughty bearing of the equerries, who appeared unexpectedly in magnificent uniforms. The visitors' book was covered with the autographs of all of the important people in the Turkish capital, and the Sultan's carriages stood constantly before the door of the hotel, awaiting their pleasure, until they became as familiar a sight as the street dogs, or as cabs in a hansom-cab rank.

And in following out the programme which had been laid down for her, the Princess Aline became even less accessible to Carlton than before, and he grew desperate and despondent.

"If the worst comes," he said to Miss Morris, "I shall tell Nolan to give an alarm of fire some night, and then I will run in and rescue her before they find out there is no fire. Or he might frighten the horses some day, and give me a chance to stop them. We might even wait until we reach Greece, and have her carried off by brigands, who would only give her up to me."

"There are no more brigands in Greece," said Miss Morris; "and besides, why do you suppose they would only give her up to you?"

"Because they would be imitation brigands," said Carlton, "and would be paid to give her up to no one else."

"Oh, you plan very well," scoffed Miss Morris, "but you don't DO anything."

Carlton was saved the necessity of doing anything that same morning, when the English captain in attendance on the Duke sent his card to Carlton's room. He came, he explained, to present the Prince's compliments, and would it be convenient for Mr. Carlton to meet the Duke that afternoon? Mr. Carlton suppressed an unseemly desire to shout, and said, after a moment's consideration, that it would. He then took the English captain down stairs to the smoking-room, and rewarded him for his agreeable message.

The Duke received Carlton in the afternoon, and greeted him most cordially, and with as much ease of manner as it is possible for a man to possess who has never enjoyed the benefits of meeting other men on an equal footing. He expressed his pleasure in knowing an artist with whose work he was so familiar, and congratulated himself on the happy accident which had brought them both to the same hotel.

"I have more than a natural interest in meeting you," said the Prince, "and for a reason which you may or may not know. I thought possibly you could help me somewhat. I have within the past few days come into the possession of two of your paintings; they are studies, rather, but to me they are even more desirable than the finished work; and I am not correct in saying that they have come to me exactly, but to my sister, the Princess Aline."

Carlton could not withhold a certain start of surprise. He had not expected that his gift would so soon have arrived, but his face showed only polite attention.

"The studies were delivered to us in London," continued the Duke. "They are of Ludwig the tragedian, and of the German Prime Minister, two most valuable works, and especially interesting to us. They came without any note or message which would inform us who had sent them, and when my people made inquiries, the dealer refused to tell them from whom they had come. He had been ordered to forward them to Grasse, but, on learning of our presence in London, sent them direct to our hotel there. Of course it is embarrassing to have so valuable a present from an anonymous friend, especially so for my sister, to whom they were addressed, and I thought that, besides the pleasure of meeting one of whose genius I am so warm an admirer, I might also learn something which would enable me to discover who our friend may be." He paused, but as Carlton said nothing, continued: "As it is now, I do not feel that I can accept the pictures; and yet I know no one to whom they can be returned, unless I send them to the dealer."

"It sounds very mysterious," said Carlton smiling; "and I am afraid I cannot help you. What work I did in Germany was sold in Berlin before I left, and in a year may have changed hands several times. The studies of which you speak are unimportant, and merely studies, and could pass from hand to hand without much record having been kept of them; but personally I am not able to give you any information which would assist you in tracing them."

"Yes," said the Duke. "Well, then, I shall keep them until I can learn more; and if we can learn nothing, I shall return them to the dealer."

Carlton met Miss Morris that afternoon in a state of great excitement. "It's come!" he cried--"it's come! I am to meet her this week. I have met her brother, and he has asked me to dine with them on Thursday night; that's the day before they leave for Athens; and he particularly mentioned that his sisters would be at the dinner, and that it would be a pleasure to present me. It seems that the eldest paints, and all of them love art for art's sake, as their father taught them to do; and, for all we know, he may make me court painter, and I shall spend the rest of my life at Grasse painting portraits of the Princess Aline, at the age of twenty-two, and at all future ages. And if he does give me a commission to paint her, I can tell you now in confidence that that picture will require more sittings than any other picture ever painted by man. Her hair will have turned white by the time it is finished, and the gown she started to pose in will have become forty years behind the fashion!"

On the morning following, Carlton and Mrs. Downs and her niece, with all the tourists in Constantinople, were placed in open carriages by their dragomans, and driven in a long procession to the Seraglio to see the Sultan's treasures. Those of them who had waited two weeks for this chance looked aggrieved at the more fortunate who had come at the eleventh hour on the last night's steamer, and seemed to think these latter had attained the privilege without sufficient effort. The ministers of the different legations--as is the harmless custom of such gentlemen--had impressed every one for whom they had obtained permission to see the treasures with the great importance of the service rendered, and had succeeded in making every one feel either especially honored or especially uncomfortable at having given them so much trouble. This sense of obligation, and the fact that the dragomans had assured the tourists that they were for the time being the guests of the Sultan, awed and depressed most of the visitors to such an extent that their manner in the long procession of carriages suggested a funeral cortege, with the Hohenwalds in front, escorted by Beys and Pashas, as chief mourners. The procession halted at the palace, and the guests of the Sultan were received by numerous effendis in single-button frock-coats and freshly ironed fezzes, who served them with glasses of water, and a huge bowl of some sweet stuff, of which every one was supposed to take a spoonful. There was at first a general fear among the Cook's tourists that there would not be enough of this to go round, which was succeeded by a greater anxiety lest they should be served twice. Some of the tourists put the sweet stuff in their mouths direct and licked the spoon, and others dropped it off the spoon into the glass of water, and stirred it about and sipped at it, and no one knew who had done the right thing, not even those who happened to have done it. Carlton and Miss Morris went out on to the terrace while this ceremony was going forward, and looked out over the great panorama of waters, with the Sea of Marmora on one side, the Golden Horn on the other, and the Bosporus at their feet. The sun was shining mildly, and the waters were stirred by great and little vessels; before them on the opposite bank rose the dark green cypresses which marked the grim cemetery of England's dead, and behind them were the great turtle-backed mosques and pencil-like minarets of the two cities, and close at hand the mosaic walls and beautiful gardens of Constantine.

"Your friends the Hohenwalds don't seem to know you this morning," she said.

"Oh yes; he spoke to me as we left the hotel," Carlton answered. "But they are on parade at present. There are a lot of their countrymen among the tourists."

"I feel rather sorry for them," Miss Morris said, looking at the group with an amused smile. "Etiquette cuts them off from so much innocent amusement. Now, you are a gentleman, and the Duke presumably is, and why should you not go over and say, 'Your Highness, I wish you would present me to your sister, whom I am to meet at dinner to-morrow night. I admire her very much,' and then you could point out the historical features to her, and show her where they have finished off a blue and green tiled wall with a rusty tin roof, and make pretty speeches to her. It wouldn't hurt her, and it would do you a lot of good. The simplest way is always the best way, it seems to me."

"Oh yes, of course," said Carlton. "Suppose he came over here and said: 'Carlton, I wish you would present me to your young American friend. I admire her very much,' I would probably say: 'Do you? Well, you will have to wait until she expresses some desire to meet you.' No; etiquette is all right in itself, only some people don't know its laws, and that is the one instance to my mind where ignorance of the law is no excuse."

Carlton left Miss Morris talking with the Secretary of the American Legation, and went to look for Mrs. Downs. When he returned he found that the young Secretary had apparently asked and obtained permission to present the Duke's equerries and some of his diplomatic confreres, who were standing now about her in an attentive semicircle, and pointing out the different palaces and points of interest. Carlton was somewhat disturbed at the sight, and reproached himself with not having presented any one to her before. He was sure now that she must have had a dull time of it; but he wished, nevertheless, that if she was to meet other men, the Secretary had allowed him to act as master of ceremonies.

"I suppose you know," that gentleman was saying as Carlton came up, "that when you pass by Abydos, on the way to Athens, you will see where Leander swam the Hellespont to meet Hero. That little white light-house is called Leander in honor of him. It makes rather an interesting contrast-- does it not?--to think of that chap swimming along in the dark, and then to find that his monument to-day is a lighthouse, with revolving lamps and electric appliances, and with ocean tramps and bridges and men-of-war around it. We have improved in our mechanism since then," he said, with an air, "but I am afraid the men of to-day don't do that sort of thing for the women of to-day."

"Then it is the men who have deteriorated," said one of the equerries, bowing to Miss Morris; "it is certainly not the women."

The two Americans looked at Miss Morris to see how she received this, but she smiled good-naturedly.

"I know a man who did more than that for a woman," said Carlton, innocently. "He crossed an ocean and several countries to meet her, and he hasn't met her yet."

Miss Morris looked at him and laughed, in the safety that no one understood him but herself.

"But he ran no danger," she answered.

"He didn't, didn't he?" said Carlton, looking at her closely and laughing. "I think he was in very great danger all the time."

"Shocking!" said Miss Morris, reprovingly; "and in her very presence, too." She knitted her brows and frowned at him. "I really believe if you were in prison you would make pretty speeches to the jailer's daughter."

"Yes," said Carlton, boldly, "or even to a woman who was a prisoner herself."

"I don't know what you mean," she said, turning away from him to the others. "How far was it that Leander swam?" she asked.

The English captain pointed out two spots on either bank, and said that the shores of Abydos were a little over that distance apart.

"As far as that?" said Miss Morris. "How much he must have cared for her!" She turned to Carlton for an answer.

"I beg your pardon," he said. He was measuring the distance between the two points with his eyes.

"I said how much he must have cared for her! You wouldn't swim that far for a girl."

"For a girl!" laughed Carlton, quickly. "I was just thinking I would do it for fifty dollars."

The English captain gave a hasty glance at the distance he had pointed out, and then turned to Carlton. "I'll take you," he said, seriously. "I'll bet you twenty pounds you can't do it." There was an easy laugh at Carlton's expense, but he only shook his head and smiled.

"Leave him alone, captain," said the American Secretary. "It seems to me I remember a story of Mr. Carlton's swimming out from Navesink to meet an ocean liner. It was about three miles, and the ocean was rather rough, and when they slowed up he asked them if it was raining in London when they left. They thought he was mad."

"Is that true, Carlton?" asked the Englishman.

"Something like it," said the American, "except that I didn't ask them if it was raining in London. I asked them for a drink, and it was they who were mad. They thought I was drowning, and slowed up to lower a boat, and when they found out I was just swimming around they were naturally angry.

"Well, I'm glad you didn't bet with me," said the captain, with a relieved laugh.

That evening, as the Englishman was leaving the smoking-room, and after he had bidden Carlton good-night, he turned back and said: "I didn't like to ask you before those men this morning, but there was something about your swimming adventure I wanted to know: Did you get that drink?"

"I did," said Carlton--"in a bottle. They nearly broke my shoulder."

As Carlton came into the breakfast-room on the morning of the day he was to meet the Princess Aline at dinner, Miss Morris was there alone, and he sat down at the same table, opposite to her. She looked at him critically, and smiled with evident amusement.

"'To-day,'" she quoted, solemnly, "'the birthday of my life has come.'"

Carlton poured out his coffee, with a shake of his head, and frowned. "Oh, you can laugh," he said, "but I didn't sleep at all last night. I lay awake making speeches to her. I know they are going to put me between the wrong sisters," he complained, "or next to one of those old ladies-in-waiting, or whatever they are."

"How are you going to begin?" said Miss Morris. "Will you tell her you have followed her from London--or from New York, rather--that you are young Lochinvar, who came out of the West, and--"

"I don't know," said Carlton, meditatively, "just how I shall begin; but I know the curtain is going to rise promptly at eight o'clock--about the time the soup comes on, I think. I don't see how she can help but be impressed a little bit. It isn't every day a man hurries around the globe on account of a girl's photograph; and she IS beautiful, isn't she?"

Miss Morris nodded her head encouragingly.

"Do you know, sometimes," said Carlton, glancing over his shoulders to see if the waiters were out of hearing, "I fancy she has noticed me. Once or twice I have turned my head in her direction without meaning to, and found her looking--well, looking my way, at least. Don't you think that is a good sign?" he asked, eagerly.

"It depends on what you call a 'good sign,'" said Miss Morris, judicially. "It is a sign you're good to look at, if that's what you want. But you probably know that already, and it's nothing to your credit. It certainly isn't a sign that a person cares for you because she prefers to look at your profile rather than at what the dragomans are trying to show her."

Carlton drew himself up stiffly. "If you knew your ALICE better," he said, with severity, "you would understand that it is not polite to make personal remarks. I ask you, as my confidante, if you think she has noticed me, and you make fun of my looks! That's not the part of a confidante."

"Noticed you!" laughed Miss Morris, scornfully. "How could she help it? You are always in the way. You are at the door whenever they go out or come in, and when we are visiting mosques and palaces you are invariably looking at her instead of the tombs and things, with a wistful far-away look, as though you saw a vision. The first time you did it, after you had turned away I saw her feel to see if her hair was all right. You quite embarrassed her."

"I didn't--I don't!" stammered Carlton, indignantly. "I wouldn't be so rude. Oh, I see I'll have to get another confidante; you are most unsympathetic and unkind." But Miss Morris showed her sympathy later in the day, when Carlton needed it sorely; for the dinner towards which he had looked with such pleasurable anticipations and lover-like misgivings did not take place. The Sultan, so the equerry informed him, had, with Oriental unexpectedness, invited the Duke to dine that night at the Palace, and the Duke, much to his expressed regret, had been forced to accept what was in the nature of a command. He sent word by his equerry, however, that the dinner to Mr. Carlton was only a pleasure deferred, and that at Athens, where he understood Carlton was also going, he hoped to have the pleasure of entertaining him and making him known to his sisters.

"He is a selfish young egoist," said Carlton to Mrs. Downs. "As if I cared whether he was at the dinner or not! Why couldn't he have fixed it so I might have dined with his sisters alone? We would never have missed him. I'll never meet her now. I know it; I feel it. Fate is against me. Now I will have to follow them on to Athens, and something will turn up there to keep me away from her. You'll see; you'll see. I wonder where they go from Athens?"

The Hohenwalds departed the next morning, and as their party had engaged all the state-rooms in the little Italian steamer, Carlton was forced to wait over for the next. He was very gloomy over his disappointment, and Miss Morris did her best to amuse him. She and her aunt were never idle now, and spent the last few days of their stay in Constantinople in the bazars or in excursions up and down the river.

"These are my last days of freedom," Miss Morris said to him once, "and I mean to make the most of them. After this there will be no more travelling for me. And I love it so!" she added, wistfully.

Carlton made no comment, but he felt a certain contemptuous pity for the young man in America who had required such a sacrifice. "She is too nice a girl to let him know she is making a sacrifice," he thought, "or giving up anything for him, but SHE won't forget it." And Carlton again commended himself for not having asked any woman to make any sacrifices for him.

They left Constantinople for Athens one moonlight night, three days after the Hohenwalds had taken their departure, and as the evening and the air were warm, they remained upon the upper deck until the boat had entered the Dardanelles. There were few passengers, and Mrs. Downs went below early, leaving Miss Morris and Carlton hanging over the rail, and looking down upon a band of Hungarian gypsies, who were playing the weird music of their country on the deck beneath them. The low receding hills lay close on either hand, and ran back so sharply from the narrow waterway that they seemed to shut in the boat from the world beyond. The moonlight showed a little mud fort or a thatched cottage on the bank fantastically, as through a mist, and from time to time as they sped forward they saw the camp-fire of a sentry, and his shadow as he passed between it and them, or stopped to cover it with wood. The night was so still that they could hear the waves in the steamer's wake washing up over the stones on either shore, and the muffled beat of the engines echoed back from either side of the valley through which they passed. There was a great lantern hanging midway from the mast, and shining down upon the lower deck. It showed a group of Greeks, Turks, and Armenians, in strange costumes, sleeping, huddled together in picturesque confusion over the bare boards, or wide-awake and voluble, smoking and chatting together in happy company. The music of the tizanes rose in notes of passionate ecstasy and sharp, unexpected bursts of melody. It ceased and began again, as though the musicians were feeling their way, and then burst out once more into shrill defiance. It stirred Carlton with a strange turbulent unrest. From the banks the night wind brought soft odors of fresh earth and of heavy foliage.

"The music of different countries," Carlton said at last, "means many different things. But it seems to me that the music of Hungary is the music of love."

Miss Morris crossed her arms comfortably on the rail, and he heard her laugh softly. "Oh no, it is not," she said, undisturbed. "It is a passionate, gusty, heady sort of love, if you like, but it's no more like the real thing than burgundy is like clear, cold, good water. It's not the real thing at all."

"I beg your pardon," said Carlton, meekly. "Of course I don't know anything about it." He had been waked out of the spell which the night and the tizanes had placed upon him as completely as though some one had shaken him sharply by the shoulder. "I bow," he said, "to your superior knowledge. I know nothing about it."

"No; you are quite right. I don't believe you do know anything about it," said the girl, "or you wouldn't have made such a comparison."

"Do you know, Miss Morris," said Carlton, seriously, "that I believe I'm not able to care for a woman as other men do--at least as some men do; it's just lacking in me, and always will be lacking. It's like an ear for music; if you haven't got it, if it isn't born in you, you'll never have it. It's not a thing you can cultivate, and I feel that it's not only a misfortune, but a fault. Now I honestly believe that I care more for the Princess Aline, whom I have never met, than many other men could care for her if they knew her well; but what they feel would last, and I have doubts from past experience that what I feel would. I don't doubt it while it exists, but it never does exist long, and so I am afraid it is going to be with me to the end of the chapter." He paused for a moment, but the girl did not answer. "I am speaking in earnest now," he added, with a rueful laugh.

"I see you are," she replied, briefly. She seemed to be considering his condition as he had described it to her, and he did not interrupt her. From below them came the notes of the waltz the gypsies played. It was full of the undercurrent of sadness that a waltz should have, and filled out what Carlton said as the music from the orchestra in a theatre heightens the effect without interrupting the words of the actor on the stage.

"It is strange," said Miss Morris. "I should have thought you were a man who would care very much and in just the right way. But I don't believe really--I'm sorry, but I don't believe you do know what love means at all."

"Oh, it isn't as bad as that," said Carlton. "I think I know what it is, and what it means to other people, but I can't feel it myself. The best idea I ever got of it--the thing that made it clear to me--was a line in a play. It seemed to express it better than any of the love-poems I ever read. It was in Shenandoah."

Miss Morris laughed.

"I beg your pardon," said Carlton.

"I beg yours," she said. "It was only the incongruity that struck me. It seemed so odd to be quoting Shenandoah here in the Dardanelles, with these queer people below us and ancient Troy on one hand--it took me by surprise, that's all. Please go on. What was it impressed you?"

"Well, the hero in the play," said Carlton, "is an officer in the Northern army, and he is lying wounded in a house near the Shenandoah Valley. The girl he loves lives in this house, and is nursing him; but she doesn't love him, because she sympathizes with the South. At least she says she doesn't love him. Both armies are forming in the valley below to begin the battle, and he sees his own regiment hurrying past to join them, So he gets up and staggers out on the stage, which is set to show the yard in front of the farm-house, and he calls for his horse to follow his men. Then the girl runs out and begs him not to go; and he asks why, what does it matter to her whether he goes or not? And she says, 'But I cannot let you go; you may be killed.' And he says again, 'What is that to you?' And she says: 'It is everything to me. I love you.' And he makes a grab at her with his wounded arm, and at that instant both armies open fire in the valley below, and the whole earth and sky seem to open and shut, and the house rocks. The girl rushes at him and crowds up against his breast, and cries: 'What is that? Oh, what is that?' and he holds her tight to him and laughs, and says: 'THAT? That's only a battle--you love me.'"

Miss Morris looked steadfastly over the side of the boat at the waters rushing by beneath, smiling to herself. Then she turned her face towards Carlton, and nodded her head at him. "I think," she said, dryly, "that you have a fair idea of what it means; a rough working-plan at least--enough to begin on."

"I said that I knew what it meant to others. I am complaining that I cannot feel it myself."

"That will come in time, no doubt," she said, encouragingly, with the air of a connoisseur; "and let me tell you," she added, "that it will be all the better for the woman that you have doubted yourself so long."

"You think so?" said Carlton, eagerly.

Miss Morris laughed at his earnestness, and left him to go below to ask her aunt to join them, but Mrs. Downs preferred to read in the saloon, and Miss Morris returned alone. She had taken off her Eton jacket and pulled on a heavy blue football sweater, and over this a reefer. The jersey clung to her and showed the lines of her figure, and emphasized the freedom and grace with which she made every movement. She looked, as she walked at his side with her hands in the pockets of her coat and with a flat sailor hat on her head, like a tall, handsome boy; but when they stopped and stood where the light fell full on her hair and the exquisite coloring of her skin, Carlton thought her face had never seemed so delicate or fair as it did then, rising from the collar of the rough jersey, and contrasted with the hat and coat of a man's attire. They paced the deck for an hour later, until every one else had left it, and at midnight were still loath to give up the beautiful night and the charm of their strange surroundings. There were long silent places in their talk, during which Carlton tramped beside her with his head half turned, looking at her and noting with an artist's eye the free light step, the erect carriage, and the unconscious beauty of her face. The captain of the steamer joined them after midnight, and falling into step, pointed out to Miss Morris where great cities had stood, where others lay buried, and where beyond the hills were the almost inaccessible monasteries of the Greek Church. The moonlight turned the banks into shadowy substances, in which the ghosts of former days seemed to make a part; and spurred by the young girl's interest, the Italian, to entertain her, called up all the legends of mythology and the stories of Roman explorers and Turkish conquerors.

"I turn in now," he said, after Miss Morris had left them. "A most charming young lady. Is it not so?" he added, waving his cigarette in a gesture which expressed the ineffectiveness of the adjective.

"Yes, very," said Carlton. "Good-night, sir."

He turned, and leaned with both elbows on the rail, and looked out at the misty banks, puffing at his cigar. Then he dropped it hissing into the water, and, stifling a yawn, looked up and down the length of the deserted deck. It seemed particularly bare and empty.

"What a pity she's engaged!" Carlton said. "She loses so much by it."

They steamed slowly into the harbor of the Piraeus at an early hour the next morning, with a flotilla of small boats filled with shrieking porters and hotel-runners at the sides. These men tossed their painters to the crew, and crawled up them like a boarding crew of pirates, running wildly about the deck, and laying violent hands on any piece of baggage they saw unclaimed. The passengers' trunks had been thrown out in a heap on the deck, and Nolan and Carlton were clambering over them, looking for their own effects, while Miss Morris stood below, as far out of the confusion as she could place herself, and pointed out the different pieces that belonged to her. As she stood there one of the hotel-runners, a burly, greasy Levantine in pursuit of a possible victim, shouldered her intentionally and roughly out of the way. He shoved her so sharply that she lost her balance and fell back against the rail. Carlton saw what had happened, and made a flying leap from the top of the pile of trunks, landing beside her, and in time to seize the escaping offender by the collar. He jerked him back off his feet.

"How dare you--" he began.

But he did not finish. He felt the tips of Miss Morris's fingers laid upon his shoulder, and her voice saying, in an annoyed tone: "Don't; please don't." And, to his surprise, his fingers lost their grip on the man's shirt, his arms dropped at his side, and his blood began to flow calmly again through his veins. Carlton was aware that he had a very quick temper. He was always engaging in street rows, as he called them, with men who he thought had imposed on him or on some one else, and though he was always ashamed of himself later, his temper had never been satisfied without a blow or an apology. Women had also touched him before, and possibly with a greater familiarity; but these had stirred him, not quieted him; and men who had laid detaining hands on him had had them beaten down for their pains. But this girl had merely touched him gently, and he had been made helpless. It was most perplexing; and while the custom-house officials were passing his luggage, he found himself rubbing his arm curiously, as though it were numb, and looking down at it with an amused smile. He did not comment on the incident, although he smiled at the recollection of his prompt obedience several times during the day. But as he was stepping into the cab to drive to Athens, he saw the offending ruffian pass, dripping with water, and muttering bitter curses. When he saw Carlton he disappeared instantly in the crowd. Carlton stepped over to where Nolan sat beside the driver on the box. "Nolan," he said, in a low voice, "isn't that the fellow who--"

"Yes, sir," said Nolan, touching his hat gravely. "He was pulling a valise one way, and the gentleman that owned it, sir, was pulling it the other, and the gentleman let go sudden, and the Italian went over backwards off the pier."

Carlton smiled grimly with secret satisfaction.

"Nolan," he said, "you're not telling the truth. You did it yourself." Nolan touched his cap and coughed consciously. There had been no detaining fingers on Nolan's arm.

III

"You are coming now, Miss Morris," exclaimed Carlton from the front of the carriage in which they were moving along the sunny road to Athens, "into a land where one restores his lost illusions. Anybody who wishes to get back his belief in beautiful things should come here to do it, just as he would go to a German sanitarium to build up his nerves or his appetite. You have only to drink in the atmosphere and you are cured. I know no better antidote than Athens for a siege of cable-cars and muddy asphalt pavements and a course of Robert Elsmeres and the Heavenly Twins. Wait until you see the statues of the young athletes in the Museum," he cried, enthusiastically, "and get a glimpse of the blue sky back of Mount Hymettus, and the moonlight some evening on the Acropolis, and you'll be convinced that nothing counts for much in this world but health and straight limbs, and tall marble pillars, and eyes trained to see only what is beautiful. Give people a love for beauty and a respect for health, Miss Morris, and the result is going to be, what they once had here, the best art and the greatest writers and satirists and poets. The same audience that applauded Euripides and Sophocles in the open theatre used to cross the road the same day to applaud the athletes who ran naked in the Olympian games, and gave them as great honor. I came here once on a walking tour with a chap who wasn't making as much of himself as he should have done, and he went away a changed man, and became a personage in the world, and you would never guess what it was that did it. He saw a statue of one of the Greek gods in the Museum which showed certain muscles that he couldn't find in his own body, and he told me he was going to train down until they did show; and he stopped drinking and loafing to do it, and took to exercising and working; and by the time the muscles showed out clear and strong he was so keen over life that he wanted to make the most of it, and, as I said, he has done it. That's what a respect for his own body did for him."

The carriage stopped at the hotel on one side of the public square of Athens, with the palace and its gardens blocking one end, and yellow houses with red roofs, and gay awnings over the cafes, surrounding it. It was a bright sunny day, and the city was clean and cool and pretty.

"Breakfast?" exclaimed Miss Morris, in answer to Carlton's inquiry; "yes, I suppose so, but I won't feel safe until I have my feet on that rock." She was standing on the steps of the hotel, looking up with expectant, eager eyes at the great Acropolis above the city.

"It has been there for a long time now," suggested Carlton, "and I think you can risk its being there for a half-hour longer."

"Well," she said, reluctantly, "but I don't wish to lose this chance. There might be an earthquake, for instance."

"We are likely to see THEM this morning," said Carlton, as he left the hotel with the ladies and drove towards the Acropolis. "Nolan has been interviewing the English maid, and she tells him they spend the greater part of their time up there on the rock. They are living very simply here, as they did in Paris; that is, for the present. On Wednesday the King gives a dinner and a reception in their honor."

"When does your dinner come off?" asked Miss Morris.

"Never," said Carlton, grimly.

"One of the reasons why I like to come back to Athens so much," said Mrs. Downs, "is because there are so few other tourists here to spoil the local color for you, and there are almost as few guides as tourists, so that you can wander around undisturbed and discover things for yourself. They don't label every fallen column, and place fences around the temples. They seem to put you on your good behavior. Then I always like to go to a place where you are as much of a curiosity to the people as they are to you. It seems to excuse your staring about you."

"A curiosity!" exclaimed Carlton; "I should say so! The last time I was here I tried to wear a pair of knickerbockers around the city, and the people stared so that I had to go back to the hotel and change them. I shouldn't have minded it so much in any other country, but I thought men who wore Jaeger underclothing and women's petticoats for a national costume might have excused so slight an eccentricity as knickerbockers. THEY had no right to throw the first stone."

The rock upon which the temples of the Acropolis are built is more of a hill than a rock. It is much steeper upon one side than the other, with a sheer fall a hundred yards broad; on the opposite side there are the rooms of the Hospital of Aesculapius and the theatres of Dionysus and Herodes Atticus. The top of the rock holds the Parthenon and the other smaller temples, or what yet remains of them, and its surface is littered with broken marble and stones and pieces of rock. The top is so closely built over that the few tourists who visit it can imagine themselves its sole occupants for a half-hour at a time. When Carlton and his friends arrived, the place appeared quite deserted. They left the carriage at the base of the rock, and climbed up to the entrance on foot.

"Now, before I go on to the Parthenon," said Miss Morris, "I want to walk around the sides, and see what is there. I shall begin with that theatre to the left, and I warn you that I mean to take my time about it. So you people who have been here before can run along by yourselves, but I mean to enjoy it leisurely. I am safe by myself here, am I not?" she asked.

"As safe as though you were in the Metropolitan Museum," said Carlton, as he and Mrs. Downs followed Miss Morris along the side of the hill towards the ruined theatre of Herodes, and stood at its top, looking down into the basin below. From their feet ran a great semicircle of marble seats, descending tier below tier to a marble pavement, and facing a great ruined wall of pillars and arches which in the past had formed the background for the actors. From the height on which they stood above the city they could see the green country stretching out for miles on every side and swimming in the warm sunlight, the dark groves of myrtle on the hills, the silver ribbon of the inland water, and the dark blue AEgean Sea. The bleating of sheep and the tinkling of the bells came up to them from the pastures below, and they imagined they could hear the shepherds piping to their flocks from one little hill-top to another.

"The country is not much changed," said Carlton. "And when you stand where we are now, you can imagine that you see the procession winding its way over the road to the Eleusinian Mysteries, with the gilded chariots, and the children carrying garlands, and the priestesses leading the bulls for the sacrifice."

"What can we imagine is going on here?" said Miss Morris, pointing with her parasol to the theatre below.

"Oh, this is much later," said Carlton. "This was built by the Romans. They used to act and to hold their public meetings here. This corresponds to the top row of our gallery, and you can imagine that you are looking down on the bent backs of hundreds of bald-headed men in white robes, listening to the speakers strutting about below there."

"I wonder how much they could hear from this height?" said Mrs. Downs.

"Well, they had that big wall for a sounding-board, and the air is so soft here that their voices should have carried easily, and I believe they wore masks with mouth-pieces, that conveyed the sound like a fireman's trumpet. If you like, I will run down there and call up to you, and you can hear how it sounded. I will speak in my natural voice first, and if that doesn't reach you, wave your parasol, and I will try it a little louder."

"Oh, do!" said Miss Morris. "It will be very good of you. I should like to hear a real speech in the theatre of Herodes," she said, as she seated herself on the edge of the marble crater.

"I'll have to speak in English," said Carlton, as he disappeared; "my Greek isn't good enough to carry that far."

Mrs. Downs seated herself beside her niece, and Carlton began scrambling down the side of the amphitheatre. The marble benches were broken in parts, and where they were perfect were covered with a fine layer of moss as smooth and soft as green velvet, so that Carlton, when he was not laboriously feeling for his next foothold with the toe of his boot, was engaged in picking spring flowers from the beds of moss and sticking them, for safe-keeping, in his button-hole. He was several minutes in making the descent, and so busily occupied in doing it that he did not look up until he had reached the level of the ground, and jumped lightly from the first row of seats to the stage, covered with moss, which lay like a heavy rug over the marble pavement. When he did look up he saw a tableau that made his heart, which was beating quickly from the exertion of the descent, stand still with consternation. The Hohenwalds had, in his short absence, descended from the entrance of the Acropolis, and had stopped on their way to the road below to look into the cool green and white basin of the theatre. At the moment Carlton looked up the Duke was standing in front of Mrs. Downs and Miss Morris, and all of the men had their hats off. Then, in pantomime, and silhouetted against the blue sky behind them, Carlton saw the Princesses advance beside their brother, and Mrs. Downs and her niece courtesied three times, and then the whole party faced about in a line and looked down at him. The meaning of the tableau was only too plain.

"Good heavens!" gasped Carlton. "Everybody's getting introduced to everybody else, and I've missed the whole thing! If they think I'm going to stay down here and amuse them, and miss all the fun myself, they are greatly mistaken." He made a mad rush for the front first row of seats; but there was a cry of remonstrance from above, and, looking up, he saw all of the men waving him back.

"Speech!" cried the young English Captain, applauding loudly, as though welcoming an actor on his first entrance. "Hats off!" he cried. "Down in front! Speech!"

"Confound that ass!" said Carlton, dropping back to the marble pavement again, and gazing impotently up at the row of figures outlined against the sky. "I must look like a bear in the bear-pit at the Zoo," he growled. "They'll be throwing buns to me next." He could see the two elder sisters talking to Mrs. Downs, who was evidently explaining his purpose in going down to the stage of the theatre, and he could see the Princess Aline bending forward, with both hands on her parasol, and smiling. The captain made a trumpet of his hands, and asked why he didn't begin.

"Hello! how are you?" Carlton called back, waving his hat at him in some embarrassment. "I wonder if I look as much like a fool as I feel?" he muttered.

"What did you say? We can't hear you," answered the captain.

"Louder! louder!" called the equerries. Carlton swore at them under his breath, and turned and gazed round the hole in which he was penned in order to make them believe that he had given up the idea of making a speech, or had ever intended doing so. He tried to think of something clever to shout back at them, and rejected "Ye men of Athens" as being too flippant, and "Friends, Countrymen, Romans," as requiring too much effort. When he looked up again the Hohenwalds were moving on their way, and as he started once more to scale the side of the theatre the Duke waved his hand at him in farewell, and gave another hand to his sisters, who disappeared with him behind the edge of the upper row of seats. Carlton turned at once and dropped into one of the marble chairs and bowed his head. When he did reach the top Miss Morris held out a sympathetic hand to him and shook her head sadly, but he could see that she was pressing her lips tightly together to keep from smiling.

"Oh, it's all very funny for you," he said, refusing her hand. "I don't believe you are in love with anybody. You don't know what it means."

They revisited the rock on the next day and on the day after, and then left Athens for an inland excursion to stay overnight. Miss Morris returned from it with the sense of having done her duty once, and by so doing having earned the right to act as she pleased in the future. What she best pleased to do was to wander about over the broad top of the Acropolis, with no serious intent of studying its historical values, but rather, as she explained it, for the simple satisfaction of feeling that she was there. She liked to stand on the edge of the low wall along its top and look out over the picture of sea and plain and mountains that lay below her. The sun shone brightly, and the wind swept by them as though they were on the bridge of an ocean steamer, and there was the added invigorating sense of pleasure that comes to us when we stand on a great height. Carlton was sitting at her feet, shielded from the wind by a fallen column, and gazing up at her with critical approval.

"You look like a sort of a 'Winged Victory' up there," he said, "with the wind blowing your skirts about and your hair coming down."

"I don't remember that the 'Winged Victory' has any hair to blow about," suggested Miss Morris.

"I'd like to paint you," continued Carlton, "just as you are standing now, only I would put you in a Greek dress; and you could stand a Greek dress better than almost any one I know. I would paint you with your head up and one hand shielding your eyes, and the other pressed against your breast. It would be stunning." He spoke enthusiastically, but in quite an impersonal tone, as though he were discussing the posing of a model.

Miss Morris jumped down from the low wall on which she had been standing, and said, simply, "Of course I should like to have you paint me very much."

Mrs. Downs looked up with interest to see if Mr. Carlton was serious.

"When?" said Carlton, vaguely. "Oh, I don't know. Of course this is entirely too nice to last, and you will be going home soon, and then when I do get back to the States you will--you will have other things to do."

"Yes," repeated Miss Morris, "I shall have something else to do besides gazing out at the AEgean Sea." She raised her head and looked across the rock for a moment with some interest. Her eyes, which had grown wistful, lighted again with amusement. "Here are your friends," she said, smiling.

"No!" exclaimed Carlton, scrambling to his feet.

"Yes," said Miss Morris. "The Duke has seen us, and is coming over here."

When Carlton had gained his feet and turned to look, his friends had separated in different directions, and were strolling about alone or in pairs among the great columns of the Parthenon. But the Duke came directly towards them, and seated himself on a low block of marble in front of the two ladies. After a word or two about the beauties of the place, he asked if they would go to the reception which the King gave to him on the day following. They answered that they should like to come very much, and the Prince expressed his satisfaction, and said that he would see that the chamberlain sent them invitations. "And you, Mr. Carlton, you will come also, I hope. I wish you to be presented to my sisters. They are only amateurs in art, but they are great admirers of your work, and they have rebuked me for not having already presented you. We were all disappointed," he continued, courteously, "at not having you to dine with us that night in Constantinople, but now I trust I shall see something of you here. You must tell us what we are to admire."

"That is very easy," said Carlton. "Everything."

"You are quite right," said the Prince, bowing to the ladies as he moved away. "It is all very beautiful."

"Well, now you certainly will meet her," said Miss Morris.

"Oh no, I won't," said Carlton, with resignation. "I have had two chances and lost them, and I'll miss this one too."

"Well, there is a chance you shouldn't miss," said Miss Morris, pointing and nodding her head. "There she is now, and all alone. She's sketching, isn't she, or taking notes? What is she doing?"

Carlton looked eagerly in the direction Miss Morris had signified, and saw the Princess Aline sitting at some distance from them, with a book on her lap. She glanced up from this now and again to look at something ahead of her, and was apparently deeply absorbed in her occupation.

"There is your opportunity," said Mrs. Downs; "and we are going back to the hotel. Shall we see you at luncheon?"

"Yes," said Carlton, "unless I get a position as drawing-master; in that case I shall be here teaching the three amateurs in art. Do you think I can do it?" he asked Miss Morris.

"Decidedly," she answered. "I have found you a most educational young person."

They went away together, and Carlton moved cautiously towards the spot where the Princess was sitting. He made a long and roundabout detour as he did so, in order to keep himself behind her. He did not mean to come so near that she would see him, but he took a certain satisfaction in looking at her when she was alone, though her loneliness was only a matter of the moment, and though he knew that her people were within a hundred yards of her. He was in consequence somewhat annoyed and surprised to see another young man dodging in and out among the pillars of the Parthenon immediately ahead of him, and to find that this young man also had his attention centred on the young girl, who sat unconsciously sketching in the foreground.

"Now what the devil can he want?" muttered Carlton, his imagination taking alarm at once. "If it would only prove to be some one who meant harm to her," he thought--"a brigand, or a beggar, who might be obligingly insolent, or even a tipsy man, what a chance it would afford for heroic action!"

With this hope he moved forward quickly but silently, hoping that the stranger might prove even to be an anarchist with a grudge against royalty. And as he advanced he had the satisfaction of seeing the Princess glance over her shoulder, and, observing the man, rise and walk quickly away towards the edge of the rock. There she seated herself with her face towards the city, and with her back firmly set against her pursuer.

"He is annoying her!" exclaimed Carlton, delightedly, as he hurried forward. "It looks as though my chance had come at last." But as he approached the stranger he saw, to his great disappointment, that he had nothing more serious to deal with than one of the international army of amateur photographers, who had been stalking the Princess as a hunter follows an elk, or as he would have stalked a race-horse or a prominent politician, or a Lord Mayor's show, everything being fish that came within the focus of his camera. A helpless statue and an equally helpless young girl were both good subjects and at his mercy. He was bending over, with an anxious expression of countenance, and focussing his camera on the back of the Princess Aline, when Carlton approached from the rear. As the young man put his finger on the button of the camera, Carlton jogged his arm with his elbow, and pushed the enthusiastic tourist to one side.

"Say," exclaimed that individual, "look where you're going, will you? You spoiled that plate."

"I'll spoil your camera if you annoy that young lady any longer," said Carlton, in a low voice.

The photographer was rapidly rewinding his roll, and the fire of pursuit was still in his eye.

"She's a Princess," he explained, in an excited whisper.

"Well," said Carlton, "even a Princess is entitled to some consideration. Besides," he said, in a more amicable tone, "you haven't a permit to photograph on the Acropolis. You know you haven't." Carlton was quite sure of this, because there were no such permits.

The amateur looked up in some dismay. "I didn't know you had to have them," he said. "Where can I get one?"

"The King may give you one," said Carlton. "He lives at the palace. If they catch you up here without a license, they will confiscate your camera and lock you up. You had better vanish before they see you."

"Thank you. I will," said the tourist, anxiously.

"Now," thought Carlton, smiling pleasantly, "when he goes to the palace with that box and asks for a permit, they'll think he is either a dynamiter or a crank, and before they are through with him his interest in photography will have sustained a severe shock."

As Carlton turned from watching the rapid flight of the photographer, he observed that the Princess had remarked it also, as she had no doubt been a witness of what had passed, even if she had not overheard all that had been said. She rose from her enforced position of refuge with a look of relief, and came directly towards Carlton along the rough path that led through the debris on the top of the Acropolis. Carlton had thought, as he watched her sitting on the wall, with her chin resting on her hand, that she would make a beautiful companion picture to the one he had wished to paint of Miss Morris--the one girl standing upright, looking fearlessly out to sea, on the top of the low wall, with the wind blowing her skirts about her, and her hair tumbled in the breeze, and the other seated, bending intently forward, as though watching for the return of a long-delayed vessel; a beautifully sad face, fine and delicate and noble, the face of a girl on the figure of a woman. And when she rose he made no effort to move away, or, indeed, to pretend not to have seen her, but stood looking at her as though he had the right to do so, and as though she must know he had that right. As she came towards him the Princess Aline did not stop, nor even shorten her steps; but as she passed opposite to him she bowed her thanks with a sweet impersonal smile and a dropping of the eyes, and continued steadily on her way.

Carlton stood for some short time looking after her, with his hat still at his side. She seemed farther from him at that moment than she had ever been before, although she had for the first time recognized him. But he knew that it was only as a human being that she had recognized him. He put on his hat, and sat down on a rock with his elbows on his knees, and filled his pipe.

"If that had been any other girl," he thought, "I would have gone up to her and said, 'Was that man annoying you?' and she would have said, 'Yes; thank you,' or something; and I would have walked along with her until we had come up to her friends, and she would have told them I had been of some slight service to her, and they would have introduced us, and all would have gone well. But because she is a Princess she cannot be approached in that way. At least she does not think so, and I have to act as she has been told I should act, and not as I think I should. After all, she is only a very beautiful girl, and she must be very tired of her cousins and grandmothers, and of not being allowed to see any one else. These royalties make a very picturesque show for the rest of us, but indeed it seems rather hard on them. A hundred years from now there will be no more kings and queens, and the writers of that day will envy us, just as the writers of this day envy the men who wrote of chivalry and tournaments, and they will have to choose their heroes from bank presidents, and their heroines from lady lawyers and girl politicians and type-writers. What a stupid world it will be then!"

The next day brought the reception to the Hohenwalds; and Carlton, entering the reading-room of the hotel on the same afternoon, found Miss Morris and her aunt there together taking tea. They both looked at him with expressions of such genuine commiseration that he stopped just as he was going to seat himself and eyed them defiantly.

"Don't tell me," he exclaimed, "that this has fallen through too!"

Miss Morris nodded her head silently.

Carlton dropped into the chair beside them, and folded his arms with a frown of grim resignation. "What is it?" he asked. "Have they postponed the reception?"

"No," Miss Morris said; "but the Princess Aline will not be there."

"Of course not," said Carlton, calmly, "of course not. May I ask why? I knew that she wouldn't be there, but I may possibly be allowed to express some curiosity."

"She turned her ankle on one of the loose stones on the Acropolis this afternoon," said Miss Morris, "and sprained it so badly that they had to carry her--"

"Who carried her?" Carlton demanded, fiercely.

"Some of her servants."

"Of course, of course!" cried Carlton. "That's the way it always will be. I was there the whole afternoon, and I didn't see her. I wasn't there to help her. It's Fate, that's what it is--Fate! There's no use in my trying to fight against Fate. Still," he added, anxiously, with a sudden access of hope, "she may be well by this evening."

"I hardly think she will," said Miss Morris, "but we will trust so."

The King's palace and gardens stretch along one end of the public park, and are but just across the street from the hotel where the Hohenwalds and the Americans were staying. As the hotel was the first building on the left of the square, Carlton could see from his windows the illuminations, and the guards of honor, and the carriages arriving and departing, and the citizens of Athens crowding the parks and peering through the iron rails into the King's garden. It was a warm night, and lighted grandly by a full moon that showed the Acropolis in silhouette against the sky, and gave a strangely theatrical look to the yellow house fronts and red roofs of the town. Every window in the broad front of the palace was illuminated, and through the open doors came the sound of music, and one without could see rows of tall servants in the King's blue and white livery, and the men of his guard in their white petticoats and black and white jackets and red caps. Carlton pulled a light coat over his evening dress, and, with an agitation he could hardly explain, walked across the street and entered the palace. The line of royalties had broken by the time he reached the ballroom, and the not over-severe etiquette of the Greek court left him free, after a bow to those who still waited to receive it, to move about as he pleased. His most earnest desire was to learn whether or not the Princess Aline was present, and with that end he clutched the English adjutant as that gentleman was hurrying past him, and asked eagerly if the Princess had recovered from her accident.

"No," said the officer; "she's able to walk about, but not to stand, and sit out a dinner, and dance, and all this sort of thing. Too bad, wasn't it?"

"Yes," said Carlton, "very bad." He released his hand from the other's arm, and dropped back among the men grouped about the doorway. His disappointment was very keen. Indeed, he had not known how much this meeting with the Princess had meant to him until he experienced this disappointment, which was succeeded by a wish to find Miss Morris, and have her sympathize and laugh with him. He became conscious, as he searched with growing impatience the faces of those passing and repassing before him, of how much the habit of going to Miss Morris for sympathy in his unlucky love-affair had grown of late upon him. He wondered what he would have done in his travels without her, and whether he should have had the interest to carry on his pursuit had she not been there to urge him on, and to mock at him when he grew fainthearted.

But when he finally did discover her he stood quite still, and for an instant doubted if it were she. The girl he saw seemed to be a more beautiful sister of the Miss Morris he knew--a taller, fairer, and more radiant personage; and he feared that it was not she, until he remembered that this was the first time he had ever seen her with her hair dressed high upon her head, and in the more distinguished accessories of a décolleté gown and train. Miss Morris had her hand on the arm of one of the equerries, who was battling good-naturedly with the crowd, and trying to draw her away from two persistent youths in diplomatic uniform who were laughing and pressing forward in close pursuit on the other side. Carlton approached her with a certain feeling of diffidence, which was most unusual to him, and asked if she were dancing.

"Mr. Carlton shall decide for me," Miss Morris said, dropping the equerry's arm and standing beside the American. "I have promised all of these gentlemen," she explained, "to dance with them, and now they won't agree as to which is to dance first. They've wasted half this waltz already in discussing it, and they make it much more difficult by saying that no matter how I decide, they will fight duels with the one I choose, which is most unpleasant for me."

"Most unpleasant for the gentleman you choose, too," suggested Carlton.

"So," continued Miss Morris, "I have decided to leave it to you."

"Well, if I am to arbitrate between the powers," said Carlton, with a glance at the three uniforms, "my decision is that as they insist on fighting duels in any event, you had better dance with me until they have settled it between them, and then the survivor can have the next dance."

"That's a very good idea," said Miss Morris; and taking Carlton's arm, she bowed to the three men and drew away.

"Mr. Carlton," said the equerry, with a bow, "has added another argument in favor of maintaining standing armies, and of not submitting questions to arbitration."

"Let's get out of this," said Carlton. "You don't want to dance, do you? Let us go where it's cool."

He led her down the stairs, and out on to the terrace. They did not speak again until they had left it, and were walking under the trees in the Queen's garden. He had noticed as they made their way through the crowd how the men and women turned to look at her and made way for her, and how utterly unconscious she was of their doing so, with that unconsciousness which comes from familiarity with such discrimination, and Carlton himself held his head a little higher with the pride and pleasure the thought gave him that he was in such friendly sympathy with so beautiful a creature. He stopped before a low stone bench that stood on the edge of the path, surrounded by a screen of tropical trees, and guarded by a marble statue. They were in deep shadow themselves, but the moonlight fell on the path at their feet, and through the trees on the other side of the path they could see the open terrace of the palace, with the dancers moving in and out of the lighted windows. The splash of a fountain came from some short distance behind them, and from time to time they heard the strains of a regimental band alternating with the softer strains of a waltz played by a group of Hungarian musicians. For a moment neither of them spoke, but sat watching the white dresses of the women and the uniforms of the men moving in and out among the trees, lighted by the lanterns hanging from the branches, and the white mist of the moon.

"Do you know," said Carlton, "I'm rather afraid of you to-night!" He paused, and watched her for a little time as she sat upright, with her hands folded on her lap.

"You are so very resplendent and queenly and altogether different," he added. The girl moved her bare shoulders slightly and leaned back against the bench.

"The Princess did not come," she said.

"No," Carlton answered, with a sudden twinge of conscience at having forgotten that fact. "That's one of the reasons I took you away from those men," he explained. "I wanted you to sympathize with me."

Miss Morris did not answer him at once. She did not seem to be in a sympathetic mood. Her manner suggested rather that she was tired and troubled.

"I need sympathy myself to-night," she said. "We received a letter after dinner that brought bad news for us. We must go home at once."

"Bad news!" exclaimed Carlton, with much concern. "From home?"

"Yes, from home," she replied; "but there is nothing wrong there; it is only bad news for us. My sister has decided to be married in June instead of July, and that cuts us out of a month on the Continent. That's all. We shall have to leave immediately--tomorrow. It seems that Mr. Abbey is able to go away sooner than he had hoped, and they are to be married on the first."

"Mr. Abbey!" exclaimed Carlton, catching at the name. "But your sister isn't going to marry him, is she?"

Miss Morris turned her head in some surprise. "Yes--why not?" she said.

"But I say!" cried Carlton, "I thought your aunt told me that YOU were going to marry Abbey; she told me so that day on the steamer when he came to see you off."

"I marry him--my aunt told you--impossible!" said Miss Morris, smiling. "She probably said that 'her niece' was going to marry him; she meant my sister. They had been engaged some time."

"Then who are YOU going to marry?" stammered Carlton.

"I am not going to marry any one," said Miss Morris.

Carlton stared at her blankly in amazement. "Well, that's most absurd!" he exclaimed.

He recognized instantly that the expression was hardly adequate, but he could not readjust his mind so suddenly to the new idea, and he remained looking at her with many confused memories rushing through his brain. A dozen questions were on his tongue. He remembered afterwards how he had noticed a servant trimming the candle in one of the orange-colored lanterns, and that he had watched him as he disappeared among the palms.

The silence lasted for so long a time that it had taken on a significance in itself which Carlton recognized. He pulled himself up with a short laugh. "Well," he remonstrated, mirthlessly, "I don't think you've treated ME very well."

"How, not treated you very well?" Miss Morris asked, settling herself more easily. She had been sitting during the pause which followed Carlton's discovery with a certain rigidity, as if she was on a strain of attention. But her tone was now as friendly as always, and held its customary suggestion of amusement. Carlton took his tone from it, although his mind was still busily occupied with incidents and words of hers that she had spoken in their past intercourse.

"Not fair in letting me think you were engaged," he said. "I've wasted so much time: I'm not half civil enough to engaged girls," he explained.

"You've been quite civil enough to us," said Miss Morris, "as a courier, philosopher, and friend. I'm very sorry we have to part company."

"Part company!" exclaimed Carlton, in sudden alarm. "But, I say, we mustn't do that."

"But we must, you see," said Miss Morris. "We must go back for the wedding, and you will have to follow the Princess Aline."

"Yes, of course," Carlton heard his own voice say. "I had forgotten the Princess Aline." But he was not thinking of what he was saying, nor of the Princess Aline. He was thinking of the many hours Miss Morris and he had been together, of the way she had looked at certain times, and of how he had caught himself watching her at others; how he had pictured the absent Mr. Abbey travelling with her later over the same route, and without a chaperon, sitting close at her side or holding her hand, and telling her just how pretty she was whenever he wished to do so, and without any fear of the consequences. He remembered how ready she had been to understand what he was going to say before he had finished saying it, and how she had always made him show the best of himself, and had caused him to leave unsaid many things that became common and unworthy when considered in the light of her judgment. He recalled how impatient he had been when she was late at dinner, and how cross he was throughout one whole day when she had kept her room. He felt with a sudden shock of delightful fear that he had grown to depend upon her, that she was the best companion he had ever known; and he remembered moments when they had been alone together at the table, or in some old palace, or during a long walk, when they had seemed to have the whole world entirely to themselves, and how he had consoled himself at such times with the thought that no matter how long she might be Abbey's wife, there had been these moments in her life which were his, with which Abbey had had nothing to do.

Carlton turned and looked at her with strange wide-open eyes, as though he saw her for the first time. He felt so sure of himself and of his love for her that the happiness of it made him tremble, and the thought that if he spoke she might answer him in the old, friendly, mocking tone of good-fellowship filled him with alarm. At that moment it seemed to Carlton that the most natural thing in the world for them to do would be to go back again together over the road they had come, seeing everything in the new light of his love for her, and so travel on and on for ever over the world, learning to love each other more and more each succeeding day, and leaving the rest of the universe to move along without them.

He leaned forward with his arm along the back of the bench, and bent his face towards hers. Her hand lay at her side, and his own closed over it, but the shock that the touch of her fingers gave him stopped and confused the words upon his tongue. He looked strangely at her, and could not find the speech he needed.

Miss Morris gave his hand a firm, friendly little pressure and drew her own away, as if he had taken hers only in an exuberance of good feeling.

"You have been very nice to us," she said, with an effort to make her tone sound kindly and approving. "And we--"

"You mustn't go; I can't let you go," said Carlton, hoarsely. There was no mistaking his tone or his earnestness now. "IF you go," he went on, breathlessly, "I must go with you."

The girl moved restlessly; she leaned forward, and drew in her breath with a slight, nervous tremor. Then she turned and faced him, almost as though she were afraid of him or of herself, and they sat so for an instant in silence. The air seemed to have grown close and heavy, and Carlton saw her dimly. In the silence he heard the splash of the fountain behind them, and the rustling of the leaves in the night wind, and the low, sighing murmur of a waltz.

He raised his head to listen, and she saw in the moonlight that he was smiling. It was as though he wished to delay any answer she might make to his last words.

"That is the waltz," he said, still speaking in a whisper, "that the gypsies played that night--" He stopped, and Miss Morris answered him by bending her head slowly in assent. It seemed to be an effort for her to even make that slight gesture.

"YOU don't remember it," said Carlton. "It meant nothing to you. I mean that night on the steamer when I told you what love meant to other people. What a fool I was!" he said, with an uncertain laugh.

"Yes, I remember it," she said--"last Thursday night, on the steamer."

"Thursday night!" exclaimed Carlton, indignantly. "Wednesday night, Tuesday night, how should I know what night of the week it was? It was the night of my life to me. That night I knew that I loved you as I had never hoped to care for any one in this world. When I told you that I did not know what love meant I felt all the time that I was lying. I knew that I loved you, and that I could never love any one else, and that I had never loved any one before; and if I had thought then you could care for me, your engagement or your promises would never have stopped my telling you so. You said that night that I would learn to love all the better, and more truly, for having doubted myself so long, and, oh, Edith," he cried, taking both her hands and holding them close in his own, "I cannot let you go now! I love you so! Don't laugh at me; don't mock at me. All the rest of my life depends on you."

And then Miss Morris laughed softly, just as he had begged her not to do, but her laughter was so full of happiness, and came so gently and sweetly, and spoke so truly of content, that though he let go of her hands with one of his, it was only that he might draw her to him, until her face touched his, and she felt the strength of his arm as he held her against his breast.

The Hohenwalds occupied the suite of rooms on the first floor of the hotel, with the privilege of using the broad balcony that reached out from it over the front entrance. And at the time when Mrs. Downs and Edith Morris and Carlton drove up to the hotel from the ball, the Princess Aline was leaning over the balcony and watching the lights go out in the upper part of the house, and the moonlight as it fell on the trees and statues in the public park below. Her foot was still in bandages, and she was wrapped in a long cloak to keep her from the cold. Inside of the open windows that led out on to the balcony her sisters were taking off their ornaments, and discussing the incidents of the night just over.

The Princess Aline, unnoticed by those below, saw Carlton help Mrs. Downs to alight from the carriage, and then give his hand to another muffled figure that followed her; and while Mrs. Downs was ascending the steps, and before the second muffled figure had left the shadow of the carriage and stepped into the moonlight, the Princess Aline saw Carlton draw her suddenly back and kiss her lightly on the cheek, and heard a protesting gasp, and saw Miss Morris pull her cloak over her head and run up the steps. Then she saw Carlton shake hands with them, and stand for a moment after they had disappeared, gazing up at the moon and fumbling in the pockets of his coat. He drew out a cigar-case and leisurely selected a cigar, and with much apparent content lighted it, and then, with his head, thrown back and his chest expanded, as though he were challenging the world, he strolled across the street and disappeared among the shadows of the deserted park.

The Princess walked back to one of the open windows, and stood there leaning against the side. "That young Mr. Carlton, the artist," she said to her sisters, "is engaged to that beautiful American girl we met the other day."

"Really!" said the elder sister. "I thought it was probable. Who told you?"

"I saw him kiss her good-night," said the Princess, stepping into the window, "as they got out of their carriage just now."

The Princess Aline stood for a moment looking thoughtfully at the floor, and then walked across the room to a little writing-desk. She unlocked a drawer in this and took from it two slips of paper, which she folded in her hand. Then she returned slowly across the room, and stepped out again on to the balcony.

One of the pieces of paper held the picture Carlton had drawn of her, and under which he had written: "This is she. Do you wonder I travelled four thousand miles to see her?" And the other was the picture of Carlton himself, which she had cut out of the catalogue of the Salon.

From the edge of the balcony where the Princess stood she could see the glimmer of Carlton's white linen and the red glow of his cigar as he strode proudly up and down the path of the public park, like a sentry keeping watch. She folded the pieces of paper together and tore them slowly into tiny fragments, and let them fall through her fingers into the street below. Then she returned again to the room, and stood looking at her sisters.

"Do you know," she said, "I think I am a little tired of travelling so much. I want to go back to Grasse." She put her hand to her, forehead and held it there for a moment. "I think I am a little homesick," said the Princess Aline.